The Mayor of Casterbridge

THOMAS HARDY

Level 5

Retold by Chris Rice
Series Editors: Andy Hopkins and Jocelyn Potter

Pearson Education Limited
Edinburgh Gate, Harlow,
Essex CM20 2JE, England
and Associated Companies throughout the world.

ISBN: 978-1-4058-6249-3

First Penguin Books edition published 2003
This edition published 2008

5 7 9 10 8 6

Text copyright © Penguin Books 2003
This edition copyright © Pearson Education Ltd 2008

Typeset by Graphicraft Ltd, Hong Kong
Set in 11/14pt Bembo
Printed in China
SWTC/05

*All rights reserved; no part of this publication may be reproduced, stored
in a retrieval system, or transmitted in any form or by any means,
electronic, mechanical, photocopying, recording or otherwise, without the
prior written permission of the Publishers.*

Published by Pearson Education Ltd

Every effort has been made to trace the copyright holders and we apologise in advance
for any unintentional omissions. We would be pleased to insert the appropriate
acknowledgement in any subsequent edition of this publication.

For a complete list of the titles available in the Pearson English Readers series, please
visit www.pearsonenglishreaders.com. Alternatively, write to your local Pearson Education
office or to Pearson English Readers Marketing Department, Pearson Education,
Edinburgh Gate, Harlow, Essex CM20 2JE, England.

Contents

		page
Introduction		v
Chapter 1	Who Will Buy My Wife?	1
Chapter 2	A Lost Relative	7
Chapter 3	A Difficult Situation	16
Chapter 4	Jealousy	21
Chapter 5	The Woman in Black	30
Chapter 6	Love at First Sight	36
Chapter 7	Rivals in Business, Rivals in Love	42
Chapter 8	A Narrow Escape	49
Chapter 9	The New Master	54
Chapter 10	The Letters	61
Chapter 11	A Royal Visit	66
Chapter 12	The Skimmity-Ride	72
Chapter 13	The Sailor's Return	75
Chapter 14	No Flowers on My Grave	81
Activities		84

Introduction

'I married when I was eighteen,' he shouted drunkenly. 'I was a fool. If I were a free man again, I'd be able to earn much more money. A man should be able to get rid of a wife if he wants to. If a farmer can sell an old horse, why can't a husband sell his wife? I'd sell mine this minute if anybody wanted to buy her.'

Michael Henchard – a young, homeless hay-cutter – is talking to a crowd of strangers in a small village where he has come to look for work. By the end of the evening, the drunken young man has sold his wife and child to a sailor and is free to live his life without the worry of responsibility. The next morning, shocked by his actions and unable to find his wife, Henchard makes a promise to himself that he will not drink alcohol for twenty years.

We next meet Henchard eighteen years later. By that time he has become a respected member of Casterbridge, a small town in the south-west of England. He is not only the town's richest businessman – he is also its mayor. But in his heart he is not a happy man. He feels ashamed of his past actions, and he is also worried: What will happen if the people of Casterbridge ever discover his terrible secret? Then, one day, a woman arrives in Casterbridge with her daughter, looking for her husband – a man who sold her to a sailor eighteen years ago. This is the beginning of a time when Henchard's character will be cruelly tested.

In the late nineteenth century, before psychology was a recognized science, people were becoming interested in the dark, secret forces that existed in their minds and hearts – that governed their behaviour and were powerful enough to destroy their lives. Stories about people whose lives were ruined by these strange, mysterious forces became very popular. One of the most famous stories from this time was Robert Louis Stevenson's *Dr Jekyll and Mr Hyde* (1886). Thomas Hardy's *The Mayor of Casterbridge* came out in the same year. It is the story of one man, Michael Henchard, and his struggle to succeed in life while fighting a losing battle with himself. Like Dr Jekyll and Mr Hyde, Henchard has two completely different sides to his personality. Although he is in many ways a strong, generous, kind man, there is a dark, dangerous side to his character which eventually destroys his life.

Henchard constantly makes the wrong choices. The story is a tragedy because Henchard is not a bad man – he wishes to be good. Strange things happen that bring him bad luck. But in the end it is his own attitude and character that destroy him.

Other characters in the novel also experience problems. A woman called Lucetta, whom Henchard wishes to marry, has difficulties that she did not create. Elizabeth-Jane, a young woman in the story, has similar difficulties. But the novel is not wholly dark. The man who is in many ways the cause of Henchard's tragedy, Donald Farfrae, succeeds in living a happy life. The novel ends well for two of its most important characters.

Thomas Hardy, one of England's best known and greatest writers, was born in Dorset, in the south-west of England, in 1840. His father was a builder and his family did not have much money, but he was encouraged to learn the violin and to be interested in books. The boy was unusually clever, learning to read almost as soon as he could walk. As a teenager he studied French, German, Latin and Greek.

When Hardy was sixteen he left school and began work as an architect's assistant. He worked as an architect for fifteen years, winning prizes for his work. In his twenties he started writing poetry and novels, and his first novel, *Desperate Remedies*, came out in 1871. In the same year he met and fell in love with a woman called Emma Gifford. During this period Hardy lived in London, where he had a busy social life. Hardy spent nearly a dozen years producing unsuccessful poetry and novels, His novel *Under the Greenwood Tree* had some success (1872) but his first real success was with *Far from the Madding Crowd* (1874). The money he earned from the story allowed him to give up architecture for writing, and to marry Emma. After a short but very busy period in London, Hardy and his wife moved back to Dorset, where he wrote *The Return of the Native* (1878).

The Mayor of Casterbridge was Thomas Hardy's tenth novel. It marked the beginning of the most productive period in his twenty-five-year career as a novelist. Many people loved the novel for its realistic descriptions and poetic style, but others thought the story was too improbable. They were also shocked by the relationships between men and women, and by its unhappy ending. These complaints were repeated when Hardy wrote his next novels, *The Woodlanders* (1887) and *Tess of the d'Urbervilles* (1891). However, Hardy was admired by many writers of the time.

During this period, Hardy and his wife regularly visited London, where they enjoyed meeting important people in society. But they were always relieved to return to Dorset, where they felt most comfortable. By now, the couple were experiencing problems with their marriage, which was unhappy. Hardy's last great novel, *Jude the Obscure* (1895), was an angry attack on marriage, which further damaged his relationship with Emma. Although some thought the book was a great work of literature, many others again complained that it was too sad and shocking. Hardy was so upset by the reaction to *Jude the Obscure* that he decided to stop writing novels completely. He had never stopped writing poetry, and believed that poetry was a higher form of art than novel writing. He began a new thirty-year career as the twentieth century's first important English poet.

In 1905, Hardy began a relationship with his secretary, Florence Dugdale. Soon afterwards, he and Emma separated. After Emma's death in 1912, Hardy wrote some of his greatest love poetry about his wife, which upset Florence Dugdale. However, she married him in 1914. In his final years, Hardy achieved the recognition that he deserved as a great novelist and poet. He died in 1928. It seemed right for the writer of such great romantic novels that Hardy's heart was buried in Emma's grave.

Queen Victoria of England, who ruled from 1837 to 1901, was a great believer in morals and the importance of the family. The whole country followed her example, and Hardy's novels examine the effect of this morality on society. Novels such as *The Mayor of Casterbridge, Tess of the D'Urbervilles* and *Jude the Obscure* show how, when morality becomes more important than kindness, it can ruin people's lives. In *Tess of the D'Urbervilles*, a man cruelly leaves his wife because, when she was younger, she had a relationship with another man; this eventually destroys her. Hardy's stories take place in small country towns, and the actions of his main characters are greatly affected by the opinions of others. In *The Mayor of Casterbridge*, for example, the townspeople are cruel to an important character in the story because they believe she has had an immoral relationship.

Hardy's novels take place in a part of England that he called Wessex. This was in fact the area where the novelist was brought up, and in *The Mayor of Casterbridge* the town of Casterbridge is based on Dorchester, Hardy's home town. The novelist often wrote about country people who do not have much money, and his great love of these people and this part of England shines through his work. His descriptions of the English countryside and country life are deservedly famous. But the nineteenth century was a period of great social and industrial change in England, and Hardy knew that the town and village life of his childhood could not remain unchanged. In his novels he showed the effect of these changes on small country towns such as Dorchester. In *The Mayor of Casterbridge*, for example, Donald Farfrae brings new agricultural machinery to the town and this starts to threaten Henchard's corn business, which uses the old agricultural methods. Hardy's novels celebrate country life but it is clear that he accepted change.

Hardy's best novels were written in the last thirty years of the nineteenth century and he can be seen as a novelist whose interests lay between the nineteenth and twentieth century. Scientific discoveries meant that people began to question the existence of God, and in his twenties Hardy stopped believing in a Creator. Instead he believed that there is a blind force that rules the universe which has no interest in human lives and desires. Bad things happen to Hardy's characters even when they do not deserve it. The universe does not care about us, Hardy seems to be saying.

In his work there is often a contrast between characters who are selfish and ruled by their feelings, and those who are more gentle and balanced. In *Far from the Madding Crowd* two men are in love with Bathsheba. Farmer Boldwood is a man with dark, violent emotions; Gabriel Oak is patient and kind. Like Henchard, Farmer Boldwood's life ends tragically. The lives of those who are selfish, weak or ruled by their feelings do not end well. Perhaps the real question that Hardy explores is this: How much are our lives and characters governed by forces that are not in our control? In some of his novels, cruel forces seem to want to destroy his characters. But in others, the answer of this great storyteller seems to be that it is possible to find happiness if we do not ask too much and, like Gabriel Oak, and Elizabeth-Jane in *The Mayor of Casterbridge*, are patient and kind.

Chapter 1 Who Will Buy My Wife?

One September evening in the 1820s, a young man and woman were walking along a dusty country road. The man was carrying a large basket filled with knives and hay-cutting tools, and the woman had a baby in her arms. Although they were obviously husband and wife, they paid no attention to each other. The man was pretending to read a song-sheet, while his wife looked straight ahead with a strange, empty look in her eyes.

For a long time the unhappy-looking couple walked side by side without speaking. The baby slept, and only the occasional weak, tired song of a bird in the evening sky broke the silence.

At last, as the sun was going down, the couple approached the village of Weydon-Priors. Distant sounds of laughter reached their ears, and the man looked up from his song-sheet with a puzzled expression.

'Is there any work here?' he asked the first person they met – an old man with a gardening fork over his shoulder.

The old man noticed the basket of hay-cutting instruments and shook his head. 'No work for hay-cutters. Not at this time of year.'

'Is there a place for us to rent? Any new cottages that have just been built, perhaps?'

The old man shook his head again. 'They don't build houses in Weydon-Priors. They just pull them down.'

He turned to leave, but the young man stopped him with one final question. 'What's all that noise? Something's happening in the village – I can hear it.'

'It's the fair, but it's almost finished now,' the man replied before continuing on his way.

The hay-cutter and his wife walked into the village until they reached the fair. The old man had been right: the serious business had already finished, and most of the animals had been taken back to their farms. However, the field was still crowded with people who were enjoying the fun and games, having late picnics with their families on the grass, or standing outside beer-tents getting drunk.

'I need a drink,' the hay-cutter said to his wife, his first words to her for several hours.

His wife pointed towards a tent with the words *Good Furmity* Sold Here* on a sign outside its entrance. 'What about in here?' she said. 'I always liked furmity.'

The man, who wanted beer not soup, looked annoyed, but he was too tired to argue. He walked ahead of his wife into the tent, where people sat around two long, wooden tables, laughing and talking. In the corner, an ugly old woman was bending over a large, hot, metal pot. The hay-cutter bought two bowls of furmity from her and sat down with his wife at one of the tables. The food was good, but the man did not seem satisfied. The old woman, who had noticed the look on his face, caught his eye and gave him a secret smile. The man understood at once, and passed her his bowl of soup, into which she secretly poured some rum. That was much better! A feeling of warm contentment came over him.

His wife, who had noticed this happening, looked annoyed at first, but she agreed to have some rum in her soup too.

The man finished his meal and immediately ordered another bowl of furmity, this time with more rum in it. His wife watched him unhappily as he became more and more drunk, but was powerless to stop him.

'Michael, we need to find somewhere to sleep tonight,' she said, as he was drinking the contents of his third bowl.

---

* furmity: an old-fashioned country soup made with wheat boiled in milk

But her husband ignored her, and began talking to the other customers around the table. By the time he finished his fourth bowl, he was very drunk, and was complaining in a loud voice about the stupidity of getting married too young.

'I married when I was eighteen,' he shouted drunkenly. 'I was a fool. If I were a free man again, I'd be able to earn much more money. A man should be able to get rid of a wife if he wants to. If a farmer can sell an old horse, why can't a husband sell his wife? I'd sell mine this minute if anybody wanted to buy her.'

'She's a good-looking woman,' one man said, looking at the hay-cutter's wife with a smile.

There were sounds of agreement from around the table, and the hay-cutter seemed surprised. He had not expected his wife to be praised in this way. 'Well,' he said at last, 'I'm not joking. If there's a man here who will offer me enough money for my wife, he can have her.'

The other people around the table looked down at their drinks or smoked their pipes in embarrassed silence. They knew that the hay-cutter was drunk, and hoped that he would change the subject. But a quarter of an hour later, with more rum inside him, he was even more serious than before.

'I'm still waiting for an offer,' he said. 'The woman's no good to me. Who'll have her?'

There was nervous laughter from around the table, but still nobody replied.

'Come on, Michael,' his wife begged. 'It's getting dark and you're talking nonsense. If you don't come with me now, I'll go without you.'

She waited, but he did not move. He kept repeating that he wanted to sell her. In the end, his wife could listen to no more.

'I think I'd prefer a different husband,' she said angrily. 'I've had enough of this one. This one doesn't please me at all.'

'Nor you me,' her husband replied. 'I'm glad we agree about

something. Gentlemen, did you hear her? My wife agrees to be sold. She can take the child if she wants to. Now stand up, Susan, and show yourself.'

A woman sitting next to her whispered, 'Don't do it. Your husband's drunk. He doesn't know what he's saying.' But the young woman was so angry with her husband that she stood up.

'Who'll make an offer for this excellent creature?' the hay-cutter asked.

Nobody answered, and his wife looked at the ground.

'Two guineas?' the man suggested, but there were still no offers. 'Three guineas?' he said, angrily raising the price. 'Four? Come on, you're missing the chance of a real bargain. All right, I won't accept a penny less than five guineas for her. For the last time, or I'll have to keep her. Five guineas — yes or no?'

'Yes,' said a loud voice.

All eyes turned towards a young sailor who had been watching, unnoticed, for several minutes from the entrance to the tent.

'You say you do?' asked the husband, staring at him.

'I say so,' replied the sailor.

'Show me your money.'

The sailor walked towards the hay-cutter and threw the money on to the table in front of him.

Everyone watched the hay-cutter in shocked silence. Until this moment, they had all believed that he was only joking. The hay-cutter seemed equally unsure of himself, surprised by his own behaviour. Did he want to sell his wife, or had it all been a harmless joke? He stared at the money in front of him, unable to make up his mind.

'Now,' said his wife, breaking the silence with her low, dry voice, 'listen to me, Michael. If you touch that money, I'll take our child and go with this man. This isn't a joke any more.'

'A joke?' her husband shouted. 'Who says it's a joke? I take

4

the money, the sailor takes you. It seems clear enough to me.'

'Only if the young woman agrees,' the sailor said.

'If she can take the child, she agrees. She said so herself.'

'Is that true?' The sailor turned to her.

The young woman looked at her husband's face and, seeing no sign of regret or pity in his eyes, said, 'It's true.'

'Good. Everything's agreed,' the hay-cutter said, taking the sailor's money. 'She can have the child, and the bargain's complete.'

'Come with me.' The sailor gave the woman a gentle smile. 'Bring the child with you.'

The woman hesitated for a moment, then she picked up the child and followed the sailor. As she reached the entrance, however, she looked back at her husband.

'Michael . . .' she began, but her husband did not look up. He was more interested in counting his money. She pulled the wedding ring from her finger and threw it across the room. It landed on the ground at her husband's feet.

The hay-cutter raised his eyes, but his wife and child had already gone. He seemed puzzled for a moment, and then a deep look of worry slowly filled his drunken face. He rose to his feet, walked unsteadily to the entrance of the tent and looked out into the lamp-lit darkness of the night.

'Where does the sailor live?' he heard a voice behind him ask.

'No one knows,' another voice replied. 'I've never seen him before. He's a stranger here.'

'I'm glad she's gone with the sailor,' said the woman who had been sitting next to Susan. 'He looked a kind man. If I'd been in her position, I would have done the same.'

'I'm not going to look for her!' the hay-cutter announced, returning angrily to his seat. 'Let her go. If she's stupid enough to believe I really wanted to sell her, she's too stupid for me!'

A short time later, the other customers began to leave. The

hay-cutter, too drunk and confused to move, rested his head on his arms and fell into a deep sleep. After tidying up her things, the furmity-woman tried to wake him, but without success. Finally, she decided to let him sleep where he was. She blew out the last candle, closed the tent door behind her, and left the foolish man alone with his drunken dreams.

The next morning, Michael woke up and slowly lifted his head. At first, he did not know where he was. He looked around him, confused by the empty tables, the smell of tobacco smoke, boiled milk and rum. Then he saw something shining on the ground next to his basket. Bending down to pick it up, he saw that it was his wife's ring, and he suddenly remembered everything. The sailor, the money on the table, the sale of his wife – he had not been dreaming. It had really happened!

'Oh God, what have I done?' he said to himself, rising to his feet and pulling the basket across his shoulder. 'I must find her.'

Moments later, he was standing outside in the bright sunlight of a beautiful September morning. The cool, fresh air cleared his head and filled him with energy. He knew what he had to do.

He walked through the empty village until he arrived at an old stone church. He went inside, fell to his knees in front of the cross, placed his right hand on the Bible and said, 'I, Michael Henchard, on this morning of the sixteenth of September, make a promise in the presence of God. I will not touch another drop of alcohol for twenty years, one year for every year that I have lived.'

With those words he kissed the Bible, left the church and began the search for his wife and child. As the days turned into weeks and weeks turned into months, he spent all the sailor's money on his search, but there was still no sign of them. Finally, in a western seaport, he heard that a woman and child fitting their description had left with a sailor and sailed for Canada.

Filled with shame, he decided to stop searching. The next day he travelled towards the south and did not stop until he reached the town of Casterbridge, more than a hundred miles away.

Chapter 2 A Lost Relative

Exactly eighteen years later, two women dressed in black were walking hand in hand along the same road into Weydon-Priors. One of the women was about forty years old, and her name was Susan Henchard. The other woman was her eighteen-year-old daughter, Elizabeth-Jane.

'Why did we waste our time coming here?' Elizabeth-Jane said, as they approached a field filled with tents and people.

'This was the exact place where I first met Newson,' her mother explained.

'Yes,' the girl said quietly. 'You've told me before.' While her mother watched the people at the fair, the girl took a card from her pocket and looked at it with a sigh. 'In memory of Richard Newson,' she read. 'Sailor, drowned at sea, in the month of November 1846, aged forty-one years.'

Mrs Newson (as we must now call her) gave her daughter an anxious look and said, 'This is also the place where I last saw the relative we're looking for – Mr Michael Henchard.'

'Who *is* he exactly?' her daughter asked. 'You've never explained it to me.'

'He is, or was – because he may be dead – a relation by marriage,' her mother replied.

'Is he a close relative?'

Mrs Newson shook her head.

'I suppose he never knew me?' the girl innocently continued.

Mrs Newson paused for a moment, then answered uncertainly, 'Of course not, Elizabeth-Jane. But come this way.' She moved on to another part of the field.

'It's no good asking for news of him in a place like this,' her daughter complained. 'Nobody here will remember anything that happened eighteen years ago.'

But her mother was not listening – she had noticed an old woman standing by a tree, bending over a pot which hung above a small fire. There was something familiar about her. When the old woman raised her head and cried in a weak voice, broken with age, 'Good furmity sold here!', Mrs Newson remembered her clearly.

'Stay here, Elizabeth,' she said. 'I'm going to talk to that old woman.'

Despite her daughter's protests, she walked off and bought a bowl of furmity from the old woman. After a long conversation with her, she returned to her daughter.

'Let's move on,' Elizabeth-Jane begged her impatiently. 'I don't know why you wanted to buy soup from that horrible old woman.'

Mrs Newson smiled and quietly replied, 'But I've learnt something about our relative, Mr Henchard. The old woman remembers him. She told me she last saw him a few years ago, living in Casterbridge. It's a long way away, but I think that's where we ought to go.'

The next morning, the two women left Weydon-Priors and began the long journey to Casterbridge. As they walked, Mrs Newson thought about her life over the last eighteen years. After Henchard had sold her, Newson had taken her to Canada, where they had lived for several years. When Elizabeth-Jane was twelve years old, the three of them had returned to England, where Newson worked as a boat-repairer. Later, he became a fisherman and spent several months a year at sea. In her simple-minded way, she had always believed that Newson was her legal husband. Then, one day, a friend had told her that hers was not an official marriage, which had shocked her greatly. She was so upset that she spoke to Newson about it as soon as he returned from sea. A period of sadness followed, after which Newson went back to sea and never returned. News reached her that he had drowned in a storm off the coast of Canada.

Mrs Newson did not want her daughter to grow up in poverty, so she decided to find Michael Henchard again. However, there was one problem which Mrs Newson did not know how to solve: her daughter still believed that Newson was her father. Should she tell her the truth about Mr Henchard? She finally decided that Michael could tell his daughter himself, if he was still alive. If not, then Elizabeth-Jane would never need to know the truth.

The first person they met as they finally reached Casterbridge was an old woman with a loaf of bread under her arm. Mrs Newson, realizing how hungry she and her daughter were, asked the old woman for directions to the nearest baker's.

'You won't find any good bread in Casterbridge,' the woman warned. 'It's the mayor's fault. He owns the biggest corn business in the area, but this year he's sold us very poor-quality grain. I've lived in Casterbridge all my life, and I've never known bread as bad as this. But you must be strangers here if you don't know that already.'

Mrs Newson thanked the woman for her help, and walked with her daughter to the town centre. There, they found crowds of people standing in the street outside a large hotel, the Golden Crown. A lot of noisy laughter could be heard coming from an upstairs window, and many townspeople had climbed steps on the opposite side of the road so that they could see what was happening in the hotel. Although she was hungry and exhausted by the long journey, Mrs Newson followed her daughter up the steps.

'What's going on?' Elizabeth-Jane asked an old man who was standing in front of her.

'You must be a stranger,' he replied, not taking his eyes from the window across the street. 'It is a great public dinner for all the important people of the town. At the end of the table you can see the mayor, Mr Henchard . . .'

'Henchard?' said Elizabeth-Jane with surprise.

Mrs Newson, who had been listening to her daughter's conversation, stared across the street, unable to believe her eyes. When she had last seen Henchard, he was a poor hay-cutter. Now he was the Mayor of Casterbridge! She did not move for several minutes until, finally, she was conscious of someone touching her sleeve. It was her daughter.

'Have you seen him, Mother?' the girl whispered.

'Yes, yes,' her mother replied. 'I've seen him, and it's enough for me. Now I want to go away and die!'

'Why?' the girl wanted to know, confused by her mother's reaction. 'He looks a friendly man. He has a kind face – and what a gentleman he is! We've come such a long way to find him.'

'I know, but this isn't what I expected. He's too powerful. I don't want to see him again.'

Elizabeth-Jane, however, refused to pay her mother any attention. She had never been so excited by anything in her whole life, and she did not want her mother to spoil things now. While her mother rested, she stared again through the window at the party in the hotel. Then, as she was watching the guests eating and drinking, she noticed something strange. Although everybody at the table was drinking wine or rum, Mr Henchard's glass was only filled with water.

'Mr Henchard never touches alcohol,' the man in front of her explained when she asked him why. 'I've heard that he promised a long time ago not to touch alcohol for twenty years. He has another two years to wait. Nobody knows why he made such a promise. Perhaps it was because he lost his wife.'

'When did he lose her?' Elizabeth-Jane asked.

'Before he came to Casterbridge. No one knows exactly how or when. But he's a strong man. It takes a lot of courage to live alone for so long and never touch a drop of alcohol. He hates alcohol so much that he doesn't even let his workers drink it.'

'Does he employ many workers?' Elizabeth-Jane asked.

'He's the most powerful man in Casterbridge. When he came here he had nothing, but now he owns the biggest wheat and corn business in the area. He's made a lot of money, but even he can make mistakes. The wheat he's just sold us is no good. I've never tasted such bad bread – it's like eating old leather. Yes, he's a powerful man, but he must be careful.'

Elizabeth-Jane watched as Mr Henchard began to tell a funny story. However, before he could finish, one of the younger guests at the table interrupted him and complained about the poor quality of the town's bread. Many people in the street heard the comment and shouted their agreement.

Henchard's face darkened. There was anger beneath the friendly, smiling surface of his expression. 'It was an accident,' he said. 'I'm making arrangements to make sure nothing like this happens again. My business has grown too large for just one man to organize. I've advertised for a corn manager.'

'But what about the wheat we've already bought?' an angry man called up from the street. 'How are you going to repay us for that?'

'If anybody knows how to change bad wheat into good, I'll gladly replace it. But unfortunately it can't be done.'

The mayor sat down and refused to answer any more questions.

While Henchard was talking, a young man had joined the crowd in the street outside the hotel. As soon as he heard the mayor's final words, he took a notebook from his pocket and quickly wrote something on one of the pages. He then tore it out and gave it to a waiter who was standing by the door.

'Take this note to the mayor at once,' he said in a Scottish accent. 'I'm staying at a small hotel along the road from here, the King of Prussia.'

The young Scotsman walked away and the waiter took the note to the mayor, who was staring in angry silence at the other guests. However, as Henchard read the note, his eyes shone with sudden interest.

Meanwhile, the crowd outside the hotel was growing smaller as people decided it was time to go home.

'It's getting late,' Elizabeth-Jane said to her mother. 'What do you want to do now?'

'We must find somewhere to spend the night,' Mrs Newson replied. 'I've seen Mr Henchard. That's all I wanted to do.'

'Perhaps you'll feel better in the morning,' Elizabeth-Jane agreed. 'I heard a young man saying that there's a smaller hotel along the road. He seemed a respectable man, so we could stay there. What do you think?'

Her mother agreed, and together they left to find a room for the night at the King of Prussia.

Mrs Newson looked at the clean white sheets on the beds in the small hotel room, and turned to her daughter with a worried look in her eyes. 'We can't afford this!' she said.

The two women were silent for several minutes, wondering what to do. Then Elizabeth-Jane had an idea. 'I know what I'll do,' she said. Without any explanation to her mother, she left the room and went downstairs to the bar.

'You seem busy here tonight,' she said to the landlady, who was sitting in an armchair by the fire, 'and my mother doesn't have much money. Could I pay for our accommodation by helping?'

The landlady was a friendly woman, and she agreed to the request. Elizabeth-Jane was soon busy running up and down the stairs, taking food to the guests in their rooms and returning dirty dishes to the kitchen. But when she took food into the room next to the one she shared with her mother, she had a surprise: the Scotsman she had seen outside the Golden Crown was lying on his bed, reading a newspaper. He did not look up when she came in, so she put his supper on the table by his bed and left the room without saying anything – but not before she had noticed what a good-looking young man he was!

An hour later, when Elizabeth-Jane was allowed to take some food upstairs for herself and her mother, she was surprised to find her mother standing with her ear pressed to the wall. She started to speak, but Mrs Newson signalled for her to be quiet.

'It's the mayor,' her mother whispered. 'He's talking to the man in the next room. Listen.'

'Sorry to interrupt your supper,' the two women heard the mayor saying. 'My name's Henchard. You wrote me this note, I believe. You must be the man who replied to my advertisement for a corn manager.'

'No,' the Scotsman replied with some surprise.

'That can't be right,' Henchard said. 'You arranged to see me tomorrow morning. You're Joshua Jopp, aren't you?'

'My name's Donald Farfrae,' the other man corrected him. 'It's true I'm in the corn business, but I've answered no advertisements and have arranged to meet no one. I'm on my way to Bristol – from there to the other side of the world. I have some inventions that will be useful to the business, and there's more chance of developing them in America.'

'America,' Henchard repeated, disappointed. 'But I was sure you were the man.'

There was silence for a moment, and then Henchard, coughing with embarrassment, said, 'If you're not the man, then I'm very grateful to you for the few words you wrote on that paper.'

'It was nothing.'

'Well, it has a great deal of importance for me just now.' The mayor explained the problems he had been having with poor-quality grain, and the trouble this had caused him with the townspeople. 'If you have a new method of curing bad corn,' he finally said, 'I'd very much like to see it.'

The Scotsman agreed to show the mayor his new invention. He took some grains of corn and a few bottles and instruments out of his bag. Henchard watched carefully as Farfrae performed a mysterious operation with his equipment. Finally, Farfrae gave Henchard some grains to taste.

'Unbelievable!' he said. 'It's almost perfect!'

'I'm glad I could help,' Farfrae replied.

'But why don't you stay here?' Henchard said. 'If you accept the job as my corn manager, I'll pay you whatever you like.'

'That's a kind offer, but I'm afraid I can't accept it. I intend to leave for Bristol in the morning.'

Farfrae refused to change his mind, despite the mayor's repeated attempts to persuade him. It was obvious that Henchard liked the man a lot. He told him many things about his past, about the time when he was a poor hay-cutter. He even embarrassed the Scotsman by saying that he reminded him of his dead brother. At last, the mayor accepted defeat and rose with a sigh from his chair.

'You're a young man,' he said, his voice filled with disappointment, 'and young men make mistakes. When I was your age, I made a terrible mistake of which I shall be ashamed until my dying day. But I must respect your wishes.'

Farfrae seemed confused by Henchard's emotional, almost affectionate, request for him to stay. He showed the mayor to the door in silence, then said, 'I'd like to stay, I really would. But I'm afraid it isn't possible. I have to go to America.'

Later that evening, Elizabeth-Jane went into the next room to collect the Scotsman's dishes. When she had taken them down to the kitchen, she stood quietly in a corner and watched the other guests, who were laughing and joking with each other. Then the young Scotsman came downstairs to join them, and he was immediately the centre of attention. Everyone was interested in his strange accent, and wanted him to sing a song about his homeland. The whole room went quiet as the young man, with a tear in his eye, sang about the mountains and rivers of Scotland. Everyone clapped loudly when he had finished, and asked him to sing again. Then they all crowded around him, asking him questions about Scotland and whether he was going to stay in Casterbridge long. They were all sorry to hear that he was leaving the next morning – and Elizabeth-Jane was especially sorry. She had realized from the young man's singing and amusing conversation that he had a sensitive soul similar to her own.

When she returned to her room, she found her mother in a strangely cheerful mood. Since Mrs Newson had heard Henchard mention his shame at a past mistake, she no longer felt afraid of meeting him.

'It was wrong for you to serve here tonight,' Mrs Newson whispered. 'If he becomes friendly with us, and then discovers what you did when you stayed here, it will embarrass him.'

But Elizabeth-Jane was only half-listening. When she heard her mother say the word 'he', she was thinking of the young Scotsman, not the mayor. 'I didn't mind serving him,' she said. 'He's so respectable and educated – far above the rest of them here.'

Meanwhile, as mother and daughter were talking, Henchard was not far away. He was walking up and down the empty street, lost in thought. He had heard the Scotsman singing about his homeland, and was thinking of how to persuade him to stay in Casterbridge.

'That young man attracts me so much,' he thought to himself. 'Perhaps it's because I'm so lonely, but I'd give anything for him to stay.'

Chapter 3 A Difficult Situation

The next morning, after breakfast, Mrs Newson decided to send Elizabeth-Jane with a message to Henchard. 'If he refuses to meet me,' she said when her daughter was ready to leave, 'tell him that we'll leave Casterbridge immediately. We don't want to cause him any trouble.'

'And if he agrees?'

'Then ask him to write me a note, saying when and how he will meet us – or *me*.'

Elizabeth-Jane walked slowly along the High Street with the message from her mother in her hand. She was in no great hurry to deliver it. It was market-day, and she was enjoying the busy activity of the streets in the warm, autumn sunshine. She was also a little nervous about meeting Mr Henchard for the first time. She did not like the feeling that she was just a poor relative hunting for a rich one.

When she finally arrived, she knocked on the door and was shown through the house into a large, beautiful garden. She was then taken through a green door into a busy yard filled with sacks of wheat. A workman directed her to an office, where she was surprised to find Mr Farfrae, the young Scotsman.

'Yes, what is it?' he asked, studying some grains of wheat in his hand.

She told him she wanted to see Mr Henchard.

'He's busy now,' Farfrae replied, not recognizing her. He handed her a chair, asked her to wait and returned to his work.

Elizabeth-Jane sat quietly, wondering what the young man was doing there. She had thought he would be on his way to America by now. What had made him change his mind? Obviously Mr Henchard had somehow persuaded him . . .

While she was thinking about these things, a man came into the room from the yard. At exactly the same moment, Henchard opened the door of his office. The other man stepped forward, hat in hand, and introduced himself to the mayor.

'I'm Joshua Jopp, sir. The new manager.'

'The new manager? He's already here,' Henchard replied.

'Already here . . . ?'

'You missed your appointment on Thursday, so I've employed another man instead.'

'But you said Thursday or Saturday,' Joshua Jopp said, pulling a letter from his pocket.

'Well, you're too late,' Henchard said. 'I'm very sorry, but I can say no more. Good day to you.'

Elizabeth-Jane watched the man called Jopp leave, then followed Henchard into his office.

'Yes, young lady?' he said, his mind on other things.

'Can I speak to you – not on business, sir?' she asked nervously.

'Yes – I suppose.'

'I've been sent to tell you, sir, that a distant relative of yours, Susan Newson, a sailor's widow, is in town. She wonders whether you would like to see her.'

At these words, Elizabeth-Jane noticed a slight change of colour in his face. 'Oh – Susan is – still alive?' he asked with difficulty.

'Yes, sir.'

'And you are her daughter?'

'Yes, sir. Her only daughter.'

'And what's your name?'

'Elizabeth-Jane Newson, sir.'

A look of relief crossed Henchard's face. Susan had obviously not told anybody the truth about their separation – not even her child. Although he had not deserved it, she had behaved kindly to him, and he felt both grateful and guilty.

'I'm extremely interested in your news,' he said at last.

Elizabeth-Jane told him everything about her mother's life with Newson, and how her 'father' had died at sea.

Henchard listened carefully, then said, 'I would like to see your mother. I'll write a short letter for you to take back to her.' Then, noticing Elizabeth-Jane's respectable but old-fashioned clothes, he added, 'I don't suppose your father left you much money?'

'Not much,' she admitted, lowering her eyes.

Henchard sat at a table and wrote a few lines. Then he took five guineas from his wallet and put them in the envelope with the letter.

'Well, I'm glad to see you here,' he said, handing her the envelope. 'We must have a long talk together – but not now.'

He took her hand as she was leaving and held it so warmly, and with such affection, that tears rose to Elizabeth-Jane's eyes.

When she returned to the hotel, she told her mother about her meeting. Then, when Elizabeth-Jane was not looking, Mrs Newson opened the letter and read:

Meet me at eight o'clock this evening, if you can, at the Roman ruins on the Budmouth Road. The place is easy to find. I can say no more now. The news upsets me. The girl doesn't seem to know anything. Please tell her nothing until I have seen you. M.H.

She smiled when she saw the money – five guineas was the same amount that Newson had paid for her all those years ago. 'This must mean,' she thought, 'that Michael intends to buy me back again!' She waited anxiously for the evening to arrive.

That evening, Henchard walked out of Casterbridge along the Budmouth Road and entered the Roman ruins. A short time later, he saw a female figure walking through the shadows towards him. She stopped in front of him, her pale, ghostly face staring at him from the darkness. Neither spoke at first. Then the woman walked up to him and rested her head on his shoulder.

Henchard took her in his arms and said in a low, uncertain voice, 'I've stopped drinking, Susan. I haven't touched a drop of alcohol for eighteen years.'

When Susan did not reply, he went on, 'I looked everywhere for you. After I discovered that you'd gone to Canada, I heard nothing more. Why didn't you let me know you were still alive?'

'I only recently realized that I wasn't really Newson's wife,' she replied. 'I'd always believed that the business between you and him was legal. I've only come to you now because I'm a widow. If he hadn't died, I wouldn't have come.'

'But I thought you knew it wasn't legal for a man to sell his wife and child. How could you be so simple-minded?'

'I don't know,' said Susan, almost crying.

'Poor, innocent girl,' Henchard said softly. 'I'm glad you're back. But you and Elizabeth-Jane cannot return openly to my house as my wife and child. Elizabeth-Jane would never forgive us if she discovered the truth. And if the people of the town found out what I'd done to you, my good name would be destroyed. No, we must act carefully.'

'I don't want to cause you any problems,' Susan said. 'Elizabeth-Jane and I will go away, if that's what you want.'

'No, no, Susan. You misunderstand me. I don't want you to leave. I've been thinking about it since this morning, and I already have a plan of action. You and Elizabeth-Jane will take a cottage in town as the widow, Mrs Newson, and her daughter. Then I will meet you, fall in love with you and ask you to marry me. You and Elizabeth-Jane can then move into my house as my wife and stepdaughter. In this way, our shameful secret will be safe, and I will have the pleasure of seeing my own child under my roof, as well as my wife. What do you think?'

'I don't want you to feel it is your duty to do this,' she replied.

However, after Henchard had spent several more minutes persuading her not to leave, she finally agreed.

'But now I must go back to Elizabeth-Jane,' she smiled, 'and tell her that our relative kindly wishes us to stay in the town.'

'Before you go,' Henchard said, 'I need to know one thing. Do you forgive me?'

Susan stopped smiling and turned away.

'No matter,' Henchard said, stepping back and allowing her to pass. 'You can judge me by my future actions, not my past.'

When he arrived home, Henchard discovered that Donald Farfrae, the new corn manager, was still in his office. He told him to stop working and invited him into the house for supper.

Farfrae had been looking forward to a quiet night alone, but he had no wish to offend his new employer. That morning, when he had tried to leave Casterbridge, Henchard was waiting for him outside the hotel. The mayor had put a fatherly arm around his shoulders and told him how much he liked him. This warmth and directness had persuaded him to stay. He already considered Henchard to be more of a friend than an employer.

After supper, the two men sat in armchairs by the fire and talked.

'I've only known you for one day,' Henchard said, 'but I already feel I can speak to you about a personal, family matter.'

He told the young man about his early life as a hay-cutter and how he had drunkenly sold his wife and child to a sailor. He described the long search for his wife and child, his promise not to drink alcohol, and the lonely but successful life that had followed. 'But now, something has happened,' he finally said, 'and I don't know what to do. My wife and child have returned.'

'Returned?' Farfrae stared at Henchard with surprise.

'This morning.'

'Then you must take them back, if that's what you want to do. Everybody will be happy and your past mistake will be completely forgotten.'

'I'd like to.' Henchard looked at Farfrae unhappily. 'But it's not as easy as that. If I do the right thing with Susan, I'll be hurting another innocent person. I met another woman two years ago while I was away on business on the island of Jersey. When I became ill, she looked after me until I was well. Unfortunately, the people on the island misunderstood our situation and believed that we were lovers. They treated her badly after I left. She was from a good family, but her life was ruined because of me. I felt guilty about this and a few months ago I wrote and asked her to marry me. She agreed, and we were planning to get married soon. But now Susan has appeared! What shall I do?'

'It's a difficult situation,' Farfrae agreed. 'But, in my opinion, there's only one thing to do. You must write to the young lady in Jersey and tell her that you can't see her again because your wife has returned.'

'Will you help me write to her and explain everything? I'm so bad at writing letters.'

'I'll be glad to,' Farfrae replied.

Chapter 4 Jealousy

At first, Henchard's visits to Susan and Elizabeth-Jane in their new cottage were short and infrequent. However, they soon became longer and more regular, and news of them quickly reached the ears of the townspeople. They did not understand how Mr Henchard, who had lived alone for so long, could be so interested in a such an ordinary-looking sailor's widow. They were even more amazed when, two months later, he announced that he was going to marry her.

After the wedding, Susan and Elizabeth-Jane moved into Henchard's house, and there began a very happy period of their lives. Elizabeth-Jane was relieved that, for the first time in her life, she and her mother did not have to worry about money. But she was a sensible girl, and she did not allow herself to become too excited by her new wealth and comfort.

One morning, while the family were having breakfast, Henchard was looking at Elizabeth-Jane's light brown hair.

'That's strange,' he said quietly. 'I always thought that our child's hair was going to be black.'

Susan waited for Elizabeth-Jane to return to her room before replying, 'Children's hair often changes colour.'

'It can get darker, I know, but it doesn't usually get lighter.'

'It can sometimes,' Susan said, blood rising to her pale cheeks.

'Anyway, Susan.' Henchard changed the subject, unaware of his wife's embarrassment. 'I have something more important to discuss with you. I'd like to have Elizabeth-Jane's name changed from Newson to Henchard. I don't like my own flesh and blood to have another man's name. I'm sure she won't mind.'

'Oh, no . . . but . . .' Susan began.

'If you can speak to her about it,' her husband interrupted her, 'I'll arrange it at once.'

Later in the day, Elizabeth-Jane told Henchard that she was not very keen on the idea of changing her name. Henchard was annoyed, but did not want to force his daughter to do anything she did not want to do. He did not mention the subject again.

From her bedroom window, Elizabeth-Jane had a good view of the busy yard behind the garden. Business was improving all the time under Donald Farfrae's management, and she saw how much her stepfather liked and respected him. She often saw him with his arm resting on the young man's shoulders, laughing loudly, chatting to him like a brother. She also noticed how serious Donald was. He rarely laughed, and sometimes seemed uncomfortable in Henchard's company.

When she walked with her mother, she was often aware that Donald stared at them both in a strange way. Perhaps he remembered her from the King of Prussia, where she had served him supper on his first night in Casterbridge? She hoped not.

One day Elizabeth-Jane received an unsigned handwritten note, asking her to go to a hay barn on a farm just outside Casterbridge. She left immediately, thinking that the request was somehow connected with her stepfather's business. When she arrived, the gates were open, but the barn was empty. She waited, and soon saw a figure approaching. It was Donald Farfrae.

'Ah, Miss Newson,' he said, touching his hat. 'I have kept the appointment. How can I help you?'

'Oh, Mr Farfrae,' she replied, confused, 'I didn't know it was you who wished to see me.'

'*I* wished to see *you*? Oh no, there seems to be some kind of mistake.'

Elizabeth showed him the unsigned note. 'Didn't you write this?'

'No I didn't.' He took a note from his pocket and showed it to her. The handwriting and the message were exactly the same as on hers. 'Isn't this your writing?'

Elizabeth-Jane shook her head.

'Then there's a third person who wants to see us both,' Donald said.

They both waited in the barn and watched the rain begin to fall. They stood next to each other in embarrassed silence for a long time, but nobody came.

'I'm afraid someone has played a trick on us,' Farfrae finally decided. 'It's a great pity to waste our time like this.'

'A great pity,' Elizabeth-Jane shyly agreed.

'Would you like me to get you an umbrella before I go?'

'Oh, no. I don't mind the rain.'

'But there are grains of wheat all over you. If they get wet, they'll ruin your dress. Let me help you.'

Elizabeth-Jane said nothing and stood very still while Donald gently blew the wheat from her clothes and hair. When he had finished, she thanked him and walked out into the rain.

◆

One evening, Henchard and Farfrae were standing in the yard, watching the workers going home. Suddenly, Henchard called out to one of the workers, 'If you're late for work again tomorrow, Abe Whittle, you'll be in serious trouble. Do you understand me?'

'Yes, sir,' the man replied, and hurried home.

The next morning, at twenty past six, Abe Whittle still had not arrived for work. Henchard swore and went straight to the man's house, where he found him in bed.

'Out of bed, and get to work at once,' he shouted.

The man jumped out of bed and started to put on his trousers, but Henchard pushed him out of the door. 'At once! No time to get dressed!'

Donald Farfrae was waiting at the hay-yard gates when Abe Whittle arrived without his trousers. 'What's this?' he said. 'Go home and put your trousers on. You can't do a day's work half-dressed like that.'

'But Mr Henchard said . . .'

'Never mind what Mr Henchard said. Go home and get dressed.'

Henchard, who had been following Abe Whittle along the street, approached Farfrae angrily. 'Who's sending the man back?' he demanded.

'I am,' Farfrae replied.

'And I say he goes to work without his trousers. It's his punishment for being late.'

'Not if I'm the manager. Either he goes home, or I leave this yard for ever.'

Henchard stared at the Scotsman for a moment, then angrily walked away. He was in a bad mood for the rest of the day, and refused to speak to anyone. When a worker asked him for advice, he said childishly, 'Ask Mr Farfrae. He's the master here!'

From that day, life for the mayor was never the same again. News of Farfrae's victory over Henchard in a public quarrel spread quickly, and people who had once asked Henchard for advice now began to ask Farfrae for his instead. Henchard was jealous of his young corn manager's increasing popularity, and began to regret that he had ever told the young man the secrets of his heart.

Things soon seemed to return to normal between the two men, and they continued to work together as closely as before. However, as time passed, people began to notice small differences in Henchard's attitude towards his corn manager. He gradually became less warm and sincere, more formal and polite.

A few weeks later, a day of public celebration was suggested for an important national event. Farfrae organized a large tent in the town centre in which there would be music and dancing for the townspeople. When he saw how excited everybody was about Farfrae's plans, Henchard decided that he too would organize some public entertainment; but his would be bigger and better than the Scotsman's! Without asking for Farfrae's advice, he suggested a day of games and activities on a hill just outside Casterbridge. He had colourful notices put up all over town advertising races and competitions with wonderful prizes. Tables filled with free food would be arranged everywhere, and there would be donkey rides for the children. Satisfied that his fair would be much better and bigger than Farfrae's small, ugly tent in the town centre, Henchard went to bed happily on the night before the event, confident that it would be a great success.

The morning came. The sky, which had been clear for the previous few days, was suddenly dark and full of cloud. At midday, the rain began to fall. A few people had bravely gathered on the hill outside the town, but by three o'clock Henchard knew that his fair was a terrible failure. He considered closing it but, as evening approached, the weather improved. He decided that the entertainment would continue. He had the tables of wet, uneaten food cleared away, and the band was called out from its shelter and told to play.

'But where is everybody?' Henchard said after half an hour had passed. Only two men and one woman were dancing to the music. 'The shops are all shut. Why don't they come?'

'They're at Farfrae's dance in the town centre,' a colleague informed him.

Henchard shut down the fair and returned home. He had tea with his wife and daughter, then went for a walk. Everybody in the street seemed to be going in the same direction, so he followed them until he arrived at a tent from which he could hear the sound of music and much laughter.

He went inside and saw a crowd of people, including Farfrae himself, dancing wildly to Scottish music. For a moment, Henchard found this funny and started to laugh, but then he noticed how popular Farfrae was with everybody, and his expression changed.

A new dance started, and many young women surrounded Farfrae, wanting to dance with him. Henchard was just turning to leave when he noticed that his wife and daughter had joined the crowd. When he saw Farfrae ignore the women around him and ask Elizabeth-Jane to dance, the shock and anger he felt was almost too much to bear.

When the dance was over, he approached his young corn manager with a false smile on his face. 'I'm going to Port-Bredy tomorrow on business,' he said. 'You can stay here and get your energy back. You'll be exhausted after all this dancing.'

Before Farfrae could reply, some other townsmen came up and spoke to Henchard.

'What's this, Henchard?' one of them smiled. 'The young man's beaten you today, hasn't he?'

'If you'd asked for this young man's advice, your fair wouldn't have been such a disaster,' a second man added.

'He'll soon be a more successful businessman than you,' a third man joked. 'You'd better be careful.'

'No,' Henchard said, staring all the time at Farfrae. 'That won't happen, because he's going to leave me soon. Isn't that right, Farfrae?'

The young man saw the hard, unpleasant look on the mayor's face and did not argue.

Elizabeth-Jane walked home alone from the dance, feeling very upset, trying to understand why her stepfather had been so angry. Lost in her thoughts, she was suddenly surprised by the sound of footsteps behind her. Turning, she saw that they belonged to Donald.

'Miss Newson, I've been looking for you everywhere,' he said. 'May I walk with you as far as the street corner?'

They walked together in silence for a few minutes, and then the young man said, 'It seems that I'm going to leave you soon.'

'Why?' Elizabeth-Jane was shocked.

'I fear that I've offended your father by dancing with you.'

'I don't think you should leave just because you've made my stepfather angry,' Elizabeth-Jane replied.

'I'll think about it,' he said. 'But now I must go. If I walk with you to your door, I'll only upset your stepfather even more. Goodnight, Miss Newson.'

Elizabeth-Jane felt a mixture of emotions – sadness, excitement, confusion – as she watched Donald Farfrae walk away into the night. Then, before she knew what she was doing, she was running towards her father's house, fighting back her tears.

♦

The news soon spread around Casterbridge that Farfrae was leaving Henchard's employment. However, he did not leave the area — he bought a small business just outside town. Elizabeth-Jane was delighted by the news until she realized that it was a corn and hay business. 'Now he'll be in direct competition with my stepfather,' she thought. 'He'll be the enemy of my family, and I'll never be able to see him again. Oh, why did he do this? Perhaps he doesn't care for me at all!'

Elizabeth-Jane was right to worry. Henchard was annoyed when he discovered what Farfrae had done, and he ordered his daughter never to see him again. He also wrote Farfrae a short, formal note, asking him to stop all contact with Elizabeth-Jane.

Farfrae did not want to upset Henchard, which was why he had opened his office as far away from town as possible. He even refused to do business with any of Henchard's customers. Henchard, however, could not forgive his old friend's disloyalty, and he treated Farfrae as his enemy. When the Scotsman's business began to grow, Henchard became even angrier. He started to ignore his former friend if they met in public, and forbade mention of his name at home.

Elizabeth-Jane obeyed her stepfather's wishes with an aching heart. Whenever she started thinking about Donald, she said to herself, 'No, Elizabeth-Jane — such dreams are not for you!'

Then something happened which helped her to forget Donald completely: her mother became ill.

Henchard sent at once for the best doctor in town and, a couple of days later, Susan's health seemed to improve. Elizabeth-Jane, who had stayed up all night to look after her mother, did not appear for breakfast on the second morning, and Henchard sat alone. While he was eating, he was surprised to receive a letter with a Jersey postmark on the envelope. His heart beat faster when he recognized the familiar handwriting — it was from Lucetta, the woman he had promised to marry. In the letter, she explained that she understood why he could not marry her, and forgave him for the problems he had caused her. But she had one last request – she wanted him to return all her letters to him.

> I am on my way to Bristol, to visit my only relative. She is rich, and I hope she will be able to help me. I shall be passing through Casterbridge on my way back. I shall be in the carriage which changes horses at the Stag Hotel at half-past five on Wednesday evening. Can you meet me there, and bring the letters with you?

When the time came, Henchard took the letters from the safe where he always kept them and took them to the Stag Hotel. He saw the carriage, but there was no sign of Lucetta. 'Perhaps she's changed her plans for some reason,' he thought. Without waiting, he returned home and locked the letters away in the safe again.

Meanwhile, Susan was growing weaker, and was soon unable to leave her bed. One day, she asked Elizabeth-Jane to bring her a pen and paper. When she was alone, she wrote a short letter, which she then locked in her desk. She had addressed it with these words: '*Mr Michael Henchard. Do not open until Elizabeth-Jane's wedding-day.*'

Every night, Elizabeth-Jane sat by her mother's bedside. One night, her mother opened her eyes and said, 'Do you remember the note that was sent to you and Mr Farfrae? The one that asked you both to go to the haybarn? And you thought that someone had been playing a joke on you?'

'Yes.'

'It was not just a stupid joke. It was done to bring you together. It was written by me.'

'Why?' Elizabeth-Jane asked with surprise.

'I . . . I wanted you to marry Mr Farfrae.'

'Oh, Mother!' The girl bent her head down to her knees. 'Why did you do that?'

29

'Well, I had a reason. You'll discover it one day, but I can't tell you now. Anyway, things have changed. Henchard hates him.'

'Perhaps they'll be friends again,' the girl said quietly.

'I don't know. I don't know.'

After this, her mother was silent. She died the following morning.

Chapter 5 The Woman in Black

Three weeks after Susan's funeral, Henchard and Elizabeth-Jane sat by the fire, talking about Newson.

'Was he a kind father?' he asked.

'Yes, sir. Very.'

'If I'd been your father, would you have cared for me as much as you cared for Richard Newson?'

'That's impossible to imagine,' she quickly replied.

Henchard stared into the fire for a long time, feeling very sad and lonely. His wife was dead, his good friend Farfrae had become his enemy, and his own daughter was still a stranger to him. He could not bear such loneliness any more, and he felt a strong desire to tell Elizabeth-Jane the truth. He rose from his chair and walked nervously around the room.

Finally, he stood behind her chair and said, 'What did your mother tell you about me?'

'She told me that you were a relative.'

'Nothing more?' The girl shook her head. 'Then I am the one who must tell you the truth. Elizabeth-Jane. I am your real father, not Richard Newson.'

Elizabeth-Jane sat so still that Henchard thought for a moment that she had stopped breathing.

'Your mother and I were man and wife when we were young,' Henchard went on. 'It was our second marriage that you saw. She only married Newson because she thought that I was dead.'

He continued talking, although he was careful not to tell her the details of their separation. Elizabeth-Jane listened to Henchard's description of his early life with her mother until, unable to control herself, she threw herself forward and started to cry.

'Don't cry,' Henchard begged, taking her hand. 'I'm your father. Why should you cry? Am I such a terrible man? I was a drinking man once, but not any more. I'll be kinder to you than *he* was. I'll do anything to make you happy. I just want you to see me as your father.'

Elizabeth-Jane stood up and tried to look at him, but she could not.

'It's all right,' Henchard said, not knowing what to do. 'I'll go away now and not see you until tomorrow, or whenever you're ready. Goodnight, my dear.'

With those words, he left the room and went upstairs to hunt for the original marriage certificate that would prove that he was Elizabeth-Jane's real father. While he was searching through his documents, he found a letter addressed to him: '*Do not open until Elizabeth-Jane's wedding-day.*' He recognized Susan's handwriting on the envelope. Without thinking, he opened it and read:

> Dear Michael, I shall be in my grave when you read this, and Elizabeth-Jane will have a home, so the whole truth can now be safely told. Elizabeth-Jane is not your Elizabeth-Jane. The child who was in my arms when you sold me died three months after I left you. The Elizabeth-Jane who is with you now is the daughter of my other husband, Richard Newson. Tell her husband of this or not – it is your decision. But please forgive, if you can, a woman you once treated badly, as she forgives you.

Henchard sat in deep shock for almost two hours, thinking about what he had just read. If this was true, he could understand why his wife had not wanted her daughter to change her name. But was it true?

Finally, he picked up a candle and went quietly into Elizabeth-Jane's bedroom. He held the candle to her face and carefully studied her features. Her skin was paler and her hair was fairer than he remembered, but there was something more important than this. The more he examined her sleeping face, the more he was reminded of Richard Newson. The similarities between the two faces were unmistakable. Suddenly, Henchard could not bear the sight of her, and he hurried away.

He stayed awake all night, trying to think of a plan of action. But when morning came, he was not prepared for what happened when he met Elizabeth-Jane in the breakfast-room. She approached him with a cheerful smile and took him by the arm.

'I've been thinking about things all night,' she said. 'I've decided that everything must be as you say. I'm going to call you Father. Mr Newson, whom my poor mother married by such a strange mistake, was very kind. But that is not the same as being one's real father. Now, Father, breakfast is ready.'

Henchard bent and kissed her cheek. He had been looking forward to this moment for a long time, but now he felt only emptiness inside.

Elizabeth-Jane could not understand her father's sudden cold attitude towards her. As the days passed, she became even more confused when he started to criticize her for small mistakes. He corrected her pronunciation, made fun of her handwriting, and was angry when he saw her helping the servants.

One day, Henchard saw her taking food and drink to Nance Mockridge, a woman who worked in the yard. In front of the woman he shouted, 'Elizabeth, come here! Why do you embarrass me by helping a common worker like this?'

Nance Mockridge, upset by his rudeness, said, 'I can tell you, Mr Michael Henchard, that she's served people worse than me!'

'What do you mean?'

'I saw her serving food and drink at The King of Prussia. Ask her if you don't believe me.'

'Is this true?' he said, staring angrily at the frightened girl.

'Yes, it's true. I worked there for one evening when my mother and I were staying there.'

Henchard walked away with a look of shame and disgust on his face and, from that day, he avoided Elizabeth-Jane as much as possible. The poor girl could not understand her father's cruel behaviour at all. As soon as she had accepted him as her father and changed her name, he had developed a strong dislike of her. Why?

She was not the type of girl, however, to waste time feeling sorry for herself. She spent her long, lonely hours reading books and educating herself. Sometimes she took a book to the graveyard where her mother was buried, and sat by her mother's grave to think.

One morning, however, as she entered the graveyard, she stopped in surprise. A woman dressed in black was standing by her mother's grave, reading the words on the gravestone. Elizabeth-Jane watched her from a distance then returned home, wondering who the woman was and where she had come from.

Henchard was already in a bad mood when she returned. His two-year period as mayor was coming to an end, and he had just learnt that he would not be offered a position as a local government official. Donald Farfrae had been chosen instead!

'Where have you been?' he asked Elizabeth-Jane angrily.

'I've been walking in the churchyard, Father, until I feel quite leery.*'

As soon as she had said the word, she put her hand to her mouth, but it was too late.

'You will not use words like that in my house!' Henchard

---

* leery: a word used by uneducated country people, meaning hungry shouted. 'People will think you work on a farm. One day I learn that you've served drinks in a hotel. Now I hear you talk like a village fool. If this continues, this house will not be big enough for both of us!'

Elizabeth-Jane went quietly up to her room and lay on her bed, still thinking about the mysterious woman she had seen in the churchyard. Henchard, meanwhile, was thinking jealously about Donald Farfrae.

'It was a mistake to stop him seeing Elizabeth-Jane,' he thought. 'If I hadn't stopped him seeing her, he would have taken her away from here and I would have been a happier man!'

He jumped up from his chair, went to his desk and wrote: '*Sir, You may continue to see Elizabeth-Jane, if you wish. On condition that you do not visit her in my house, I will not stand in your way. Yours, M. Henchard.*'

The following morning, Elizabeth-Jane was sitting on a seat by her mother's grave, feeling sorry for herself.

'Oh, why can't I be dead, like my dear mother?' she said aloud.

Suddenly, something made her look round. A face was bending over her from behind the seat; it was the face of the mysterious woman she had seen yesterday.

'Yes, I heard you,' the woman said, noticing Elizabeth-Jane's confusion. 'Why are you so sad?'

'I can't tell you,' Elizabeth-Jane replied, putting her hands to her face to cover her embarrassment.

Moments later, the woman was sitting next to her. 'I think I can guess,' she said, nodding in the direction of the gravestone. 'That was your mother, wasn't it?'

There was something so warm and friendly about the stranger's face that Elizabeth-Jane trusted her immediately.

'Yes,' she admitted. 'It was my mother. My only friend.'

'But your father, Mr Henchard. He's living?'

'Yes, he's living.'

'Isn't he kind to you?'

'I've no wish to complain of him.'

'There's been a disagreement?'

'A little.'

'Perhaps it was your fault,' the stranger suggested.

'It was – in many ways,' sighed Elizabeth-Jane. 'I served a worker food and drink, and I used the word "leery".'

The other woman smiled warmly at this reply. 'Your father seems to be a hot-tempered man – perhaps a little ambitious and proud,' she said. 'But not a bad man.'

'Oh no, certainly not *bad*,' Elizabeth-Jane agreed. 'And he hasn't been unkind to me until recently – since Mother died. As you say, it's probably my fault for making so many mistakes. But, you see, I've lived all my life in poverty. This way of life is new to me, and it's hard to change the way I act and speak.'

Soon, Elizabeth-Jane was telling the other woman everything about her life, and was pleasantly surprised to see that her new friend was not shocked. This made her more cheerful, but then she suddenly remembered that it was time to return home.

'I don't know how to go back,' she said quietly. 'I have dreams of leaving, but I have nowhere to go. What can I do?'

'I might be able to help you,' her friend replied. 'I shall soon want somebody to live in my house, partly as housekeeper, partly as a friend. Would you be interested?'

'Oh, yes,' said Elizabeth-Jane, her eyes shining with excitement. 'But where do you live, madam?'

'I've just bought a house in Casterbridge. I shall be moving in this afternoon. It's the old stone house next to the market. Now, will you think about my offer for a few days? If you're still interested, you can meet me here the first fine day next week.'

Elizabeth-Jane eagerly agreed, and the two women said goodbye at the churchyard gates.

Chapter 6 Love at First Sight

Elizabeth-Jane was surprised by Henchard's reaction to the news that she was leaving – he was friendlier to her than he had been for many weeks. She was even more surprised when he offered her a small income to help her survive on the low wages she would be paid.

We need to go back to the previous night in order to understand Henchard's change of attitude towards Elizabeth-Jane. He had received a letter by hand, and had recognized Lucetta's handwriting on the envelope:

> My dear Mr Henchard, Do not be surprised, but I have come to live in Casterbridge. My good aunt Templeman, who lived in Bristol, died and left me some of her property. I have taken her name in order to escape from my unhappy past. I have rented High Street Hall, near the market square, which will be very convenient for you to visit. I heard about the death of your wife, so now I am asking you to keep the promise you made me before she returned. I hope you feel the same way as I do, and we can meet in a day or two. Yours, Lucetta.

His good mood continued until Elizabeth-Jane was getting into the carriage, ready to leave.

'You haven't told me your new address,' he reminded her.

'It isn't far away,' she smiled. 'It's High Street Hall, the old stone house by the market square.'

'Where?' Henchard's face froze with disbelief.

She repeated the words to him, but he neither spoke nor moved. Ignoring her friendly goodbye, he coldly watched the carriage drive her away.

A few days after Elizabeth-Jane had left, Henchard received another letter from Lucetta:

You are probably aware of the arrangement I have made with your daughter. Do you understand, Michael, why I have done it? It will give you an excuse to visit my house. She is a dear, good girl, and she thinks you have treated her unfairly. I am sure you did not treat her this way on purpose. I look forward to your first visit. Yours always, Lucetta.

Henchard visited Lucetta's house but was told that Miss Templeman was busy. Annoyed, he returned home and decided not to visit her the next day.

Lucetta waited for Henchard to call the following day, but she did not tell Elizabeth-Jane that the person she expected was her father. While she was waiting, she sat with Elizabeth-Jane by an upstairs window and looked down at the busy market.

Elizabeth-Jane could see the top of her father's hat moving around the crowd, but was not aware that Lucetta was watching the same thing with even more interest than she was. Then she noticed Donald Farfrae standing by a tree, talking to a farmer.

'Are you particularly interested in anyone out there?' Lucetta asked.

'Oh, no,' Elizabeth-Jane said, her cheeks going red.

Lucetta looked hard at her. 'Quite sure?'

'Absolutely.'

Lucetta looked out of the window again, impatiently waiting for Henchard to call. When he did not, she sighed. 'Perhaps he's too busy,' she thought. 'Perhaps he'll come on Sunday.'

The days passed, and Lucetta dressed in her best clothes every morning, but there was still no sign of Henchard. On Thursday morning, Lucetta said to Elizabeth-Jane, 'I imagine your father may call to see you today?'

Elizabeth-Jane shook her head. 'He won't come. After all the quarrels we've had, I'm sure he doesn't want to visit any place where he might see *me*.'

At first, Lucetta went very quiet. Then, without warning, she burst into tears. When she had recovered, there was a change in her attitude. She asked Elizabeth-Jane, in a cool voice, to do a few jobs for her in town. Elizabeth-Jane obeyed, puzzled by the sudden change in her friend's behaviour.

Ten minutes after she had gone, Lucetta sent one of her servants to Henchard's with a note:

Dear Michael, You will be in the market square today, as usual, so please visit me. I am disappointed that you have not come before. Your daughter's presence here may be the reason for this; I have therefore sent her away for the morning. Lucetta.

She then sat down and waited for him to call. Some time later, a man's step was heard on the stairs. However, the man who entered her room was years younger than Henchard, and much more handsome!

'Forgive me,' Donald Farfrae said. 'I came here expecting to find Miss Henchard. If I had known she was not here, I would not have come in so rudely. Please excuse me.'

Farfrae moved towards the door, but Lucetta stopped him. 'No,' she said. 'Please sit down. Miss Henchard will be here soon.'

He hesitated for a moment, then sat down opposite Lucetta. For several minutes, they talked politely about unimportant things. Then Farfrae told her about a recent business success which had brought him a large amount of money and Lucetta talked about her life of loneliness. Farfrae enjoyed talking to her so much that he soon forgot his original reason for coming. Eventually, he rose to his feet.

'I've suddenly remembered,' he said, 'I have to meet someone at twelve o'clock in the market, and I'm already very late.'

Lucetta, who was grateful for the company of such a good-looking young man, tried to persuade him to stay. He paused for a moment, and looked anxiously out of the window at the market, where the farmer was waiting for him. The farmer looked annoyed, and was walking across the street to where Henchard was standing.

'I'd like to stay, but I'm afraid I must go,' he decided. 'I must look after my business. But I'll come another time, if I may?'

'Certainly,' she agreed. 'I look forward to seeing you again.'

By the time Farfrae left the house, he had completely forgotten about Elizabeth-Jane. His head was filled with thoughts of Lucetta, and his heart was filled with a mysterious joy.

Lucetta, meanwhile, had found his combination of youth, good looks and gentlemanly behaviour extremely attractive. She watched from her window, filled with desire, as Farfrae walked through the crowd of farmers in the square. Finally he entered the market building, and she could see him no more.

Three minutes later there was a loud knock on the front door. A servant announced that Mr Henchard was downstairs.

'Tell him I have a headache and I'll see him another time,' Lucetta replied.

The message was taken down and she sighed with relief when she heard the door close. She needed time alone to think. She had come to Casterbridge to reawaken Henchard's interest in her, but she was no longer interested in him.

There had also been another important change. Earlier that morning, she had considered asking Elizabeth-Jane to leave the house, but now she suddenly wanted the opposite! She realized that Elizabeth-Jane's presence in her house would be a useful way of keeping Henchard away.

When Elizabeth-Jane finally returned, unaware of what had happened in her absence, Lucetta stood up and greeted her warmly.

'I'm so glad you've come back,' she said.

After Lucetta's strange coolness towards her earlier that morning, Elizabeth-Jane was delighted to see this return to normal friendliness.

The following Saturday, Lucetta and Elizabeth-Jane joined a large crowd of people who had gathered in the market square to look at a new piece of brightly coloured farming machinery.

'It looks like a kind of agricultural piano,' Lucetta said. 'I wonder who thought of introducing it here?'

Both women immediately thought of Donald Farfrae, but neither of them said what was on their mind. They studied the machine in silence, amazed by its rows of strange tubes and levers. Suddenly, their exploration of the machine was interrupted by a familiar voice:

'Good morning Elizabeth-Jane.' It was Henchard.

Elizabeth-Jane was embarrassed, and said the first thing that came into her head. 'This is the lady I live with, Father — Miss Templeman.'

Henchard raised his hat politely.

'I am happy to meet you,' Lucetta said. 'We were looking at this machine. Isn't it strange? I wonder who brought it here?'

'Oh, don't ask me, ma'am*!' said Henchard. 'It was brought here by one of our machinists on the advice of a stupid young man ...' but he stopped in mid-sentence when he noticed an anxious look on Elizabeth-Jane's face.

As he turned to go away, Elizabeth-Jane heard him whisper something to Lucetta: 'You refused to see me!' At first, she thought she had imagined it. Had her father been talking to somebody else — a farmer perhaps?

As Henchard walked away towards the market building, Lucetta seemed strangely silent. Then the sound of someone singing a Scottish song could be heard, and both women looked up. Donald Farfrae was standing proudly by the new machine.

'Do you like it?' He spoke directly to Lucetta, ignoring

---

* ma'am: short form of 'madam'

Elizabeth-Jane. 'It will modernize planting corn-seed beyond your imagination! It will do the work with greater speed and efficiency than people can. Machines like this are already very common in the east and north of England.'

'Is it yours?' Lucetta asked him.

'Oh, no, madam. I only recommended that it should be bought.'

The two women returned to the house, and Lucetta was especially kind to Elizabeth-Jane that day. They sat together at the upstairs window, watching the activity in the market. Something about the look on Lucetta's face, however, made Elizabeth-Jane think about Donald Farfrae. She remembered the way he had looked at Lucetta, not at her, and from that moment she began to observe her employer and friend more carefully.

A few days later, Lucetta put on a beautiful red dress and prepared to go out. As she was leaving, her eyes met Elizabeth-Jane's, and Elizabeth-Jane somehow knew that her friend was going to meet Donald. When she came back later that day, Lucetta's eyes were shining and her cheeks were as red as fire. Elizabeth-Jane knew that she had been right.

'You've seen Mr Farfrae, haven't you?' she said shyly.

'Yes,' said Lucetta, feverish with excitement. 'How did you know?'

Elizabeth-Jane did not reply, and Lucetta went to her room. The next morning, she told Elizabeth-Jane a story about a friend who had promised to marry one man but had fallen in love with another. Elizabeth-Jane knew that she was really talking about herself, and did not encourage the discussion. That night, she went to bed unhappily.

'Why did she invent that stupid story about a friend?' she wondered as she lay in bed, her eyes filling with tears. 'I know she was really talking about herself and Donald. Why didn't she trust me with the truth?'

Chapter 7   Rivals in Business, Rivals in Love

Farfrae visited Lucetta with increasing regularity. During these visits, Elizabeth-Jane was completely ignored and always left the room as soon as she could, filled with sadness at the change in Donald's attitude towards her.

At the same time, Henchard's interest in Lucetta was growing. Once he had only felt a warm pity for her, but now her wealth and independence excited him. As she still did not contact him, he decided to visit her while Elizabeth-Jane was out.

'It's so kind of you to call,' Lucetta said, smiling politely.

'Of course I've called, Lucetta,' he replied, hurt by her unenthusiastic welcome. 'I've come to tell you that I'm ready to marry you. You can choose the date of the wedding.'

'It's still too early,' she said, looking away with embarrassment.

'Yes, I suppose it is. But I feel I must do my duty towards you, as I've always promised. Since my wife is now dead, there's no reason to delay things. I was going to call earlier but . . .' His voice fell as he looked around him at the beautiful, expensive furniture in the room. 'You can imagine how all this money you suddenly received from your aunt makes me feel.'

'What do you mean?'

'You may or may not be grateful,' Henchard went on, increasingly annoyed by her coldness. 'Perhaps your sudden wealth makes you think I'm not enough of a gentleman for you, but my words are sincere.'

'That's a rather rude way of speaking to me,' Lucetta protested.

'Not at all! But I don't want to quarrel. I came here with an honest offer of marriage for you. Do you accept it or not?'

'Let's not decide immediately,' Lucetta said. 'I think we should let our friendship develop more slowly. The people of Casterbridge will think it is strange if we act too quickly.'

'I see,' Henchard said, his eyes dark with anger. 'You come to live in Casterbridge but now you're here, you refuse my offer of marriage.' With those words, he left the room.

The next day, Henchard wanted to visit Lucetta again, but she sent him a message to say she was too busy. This happened for several more days, but Henchard was not the kind of man to accept defeat, and he finally succeeded in seeing her. Lucetta offered him tea, and he sat talking to her while Elizabeth-Jane quietly listened. Their conversation, however, was soon interrupted by a knock on the door and Donald Farfrae walked in. Henchard noticed the look of embarrassment on Lucetta's face, and felt strangely jealous. He had not realized that Lucetta and Farfrae knew each other.

Elizabeth-Jane watched from a distance as the three people sat stiffly side by side at the table, smiling with exaggerated politeness, struggling to hide their secret thoughts and hidden desires. 'How stupid the three of them are,' she thought.

When Henchard left, his heart was filled with jealousy. He had no proof, but he was certain that Farfrae was not just his rival in business – he was also his rival in love! 'I must take immediate action before he takes everything from me,' he thought.

The next day he hired a new corn manager. He chose Jopp, the man he had intended to employ before Farfrae arrived, because he knew that Jopp, too, hated Farfrae. He also knew that Jopp had once lived on the island of Jersey, and was the only other person in Casterbridge who knew about Lucetta's past. Together, they planned to put Farfrae out of business by selling their own corn more cheaply. They also planned to buy as much corn as possible before the harvest.

'The forecast's not good,' Jopp said. 'If the weather's like this in August, it will be a bad harvest. The price of corn will go up and we can sell all our corn for a large profit. We'll make so much money that we'll be able to cut our prices, and Mr Farfrae will go out of business.'

Henchard liked the idea, and he spent a long time talking to people who knew a lot about the weather. All their forecasts suggested that there was going to be heavy rain in August, and the harvest was going to be bad.

Henchard bought so much grain that the whole town began talking about it. However, as soon as he had filled his barns, an unexpected thing happened. The direction of the wind changed, and the sun began to shine. It shone all through August, and the farmers of Casterbridge enjoyed a wonderful harvest. The price of corn fell lower than the price that Henchard had paid for his. As a result, nobody bought his corn, and he soon found himself in debt. The good weather continued, and his debts increased until he was unable to pay them.

Finally, he was forced to sell a lot of his property to the bank. Returning to his yard, the first person he saw was Jopp.

'A lovely day, sir,' his corn manager greeted him.

'A lovely day?' Henchard shouted angrily. 'It would have been if I hadn't listened to your advice!'

The poor man protested his innocence, but Henchard was unforgiving. 'I don't need your services any more. Goodbye!'

Jopp went pale as he watched Henchard walk away. 'You'll be sorry for this, sir,' he said quietly. 'As sorry as a man can be.'

The good harvest continued for three more days, then the wind changed direction and rain began to fall. If Henchard had waited three more days before selling his property, he would not have lost so much money. But, as we have already seen, he was an impatient man, and this was not the first time that his emotions had destroyed his sense of judgement.

While Henchard watched the change in the weather and cursed his bad luck, Farfrae's business grew increasingly successful. When prices had fallen in the good weather, he had bought large amounts of corn, which he now sold for an enormous profit.

'He'll soon be mayor!' Henchard thought bitterly when he saw his enemy's success.

♦

One dark September night, angry voices in the street brought Lucetta and Elizabeth-Jane to the window. The road was blocked by two hay-wagons, and the drivers were shouting at each other to get out of the way. The situation was made worse because one of the drivers worked for Henchard, the other for Farfrae.

'You did this on purpose!' Farfrae's driver said. 'You can hear my horses' bells half a mile away!'

'If you'd been watching the road, you'd have seen me coming!' the other man replied.

According to the strict rules of the road, Henchard's man was in the wrong, and he finally attempted to move out of the way. As he did so, however, he drove backwards into the wall of the church, and the hay in his wagon fell across the road.

The two men started fighting, and were only separated when Henchard arrived. When he saw the state of his wagon and all the hay lying in the road, he shouted angrily at Farfrae's man.

'I saw it all, Mr Henchard,' Lucetta called from the doorway of her house, 'and your man was most in the wrong.'

'Oh, I didn't notice you, Miss Templeman,' he said, interrupting his attack on the driver. 'My man in the wrong? I beg your pardon, but I must disagree . . .'

'No, I saw it, too,' said Elizabeth-Jane, who had joined Lucetta in the doorway. 'It was not the other man's fault.'

'You can't trust *their* opinion,' whispered Henchard's man.

'Why not?' Henchard said sharply.

'All the women like Farfrae. He enters a woman's heart like a rat enters a sheep's brain.'

'Do you realize you are talking about the woman I intend to

marry? Farfrae is well aware of that. He's good at business, but he would not cheat in matters of the heart.'

He turned to speak to Lucetta again, but she had already disappeared inside her house and shut the door.

'Make sure that nobody damages the hay tonight, Stubberd,' Henchard said to the old policeman who had just arrived on the scene. 'If any carriage or wagon wants to pass this way, tell them to use a back street. Oh, before I forget – are there any cases at the town hall tomorrow?'

'Yes, sir. An old homeless woman was arrested for being drunk and using bad language outside the church.'

'The new mayor's out of town, isn't he?'

'He is, sir.'

'Then I'll be there. Don't forget to look after my hay until tomorrow. Goodnight to you.'

Henchard, upset by his man's earlier comments about Farfrae, wanted to speak to Lucetta. He knocked on her door, but was told by a servant that Miss Templeman was unable to see him because she had an appointment in town. He crossed the street and, from the safety of the shadows, he watched Lucetta's house. Candles were moving around an upstairs bedroom, and it was obvious that she was preparing for her appointment. As the church clock struck nine o'clock, Farfrae appeared in front of the house and knocked at the door. Lucetta came out to meet him, and together they walked along the dark side streets until they reached the fields outside town. Henchard followed them at a safe distance, and listened from the shadows as Farfrae told Lucetta how much he admired her. Lucetta smiled, and replied that she loved nobody else. The conversation continued for a few minutes, then Farfrae walked on alone towards the fields, where workers were still harvesting wheat by moonlight.

Henchard followed Lucetta home. He was in such a state of

confusion and anger that he forgot his manners, and he followed her into the house without knocking.

'It's past ten o'clock!' Lucetta said, her eyes flashing with anger when he followed her into the sitting room. 'You have no right to surprise me like this.'

'Perhaps I don't have the right, but I have the excuse. I called an hour ago, but you refused to see me. I've come to remind you of a small matter between us, which I think you've forgotten.'

She sank into a chair and turned pale. 'I don't want to hear it,' she sighed. 'If you had offered to marry me because you loved me, I would probably have accepted. But when I learnt that you planned to marry me because you pitied me — because you felt it was your duty — I did not care for you as deeply as before.'

'Why did you come here to find me, then?'

'I still thought that marriage to you was the best way to lose the shame of my past.'

'So what has changed your mind now?'

She paused for a moment, then said, 'I was a poor girl then. Now my circumstances have changed.'

'That's true, and it makes the situation difficult for me. But I don't want to touch your money. Besides, that argument has nothing in it. The man you're thinking of is no better than me.'

'If you were as good as he, you would leave me!' she cried, her voice filled with emotion.

'You cannot refuse me,' Henchard raised his voice, the obvious strength of Lucetta's feelings for Farfrae only increasing the strength of his own desire to defeat them. 'Unless you promise now to be my wife, I'll make sure the whole town knows the secret of our past.'

Lucetta's face was filled with desperation, but Henchard looked at her without pity. After a long pause, she rang the bell and asked for Elizabeth-Jane to be brought to the room.

'Elizabeth-Jane,' Henchard said, taking her hand as soon as she had entered the room. 'I want you to hear this.' And, turning to Lucetta, 'Will you, or will you not, marry me?'

'If you wish it, I must agree.'

'You say yes?'

'I do.'

As soon as she had said these words, she fainted.

'Don't make her do this if she doesn't want to, Father,' Elizabeth-Jane said, kneeling down to comfort her. 'It's cruel.'

'Don't be so simple-minded,' Henchard said. 'This promise will leave him free for you, if you still want him.'

At this, Lucetta opened her eyes without warning. 'Him? Who are you talking about?'

'Nobody,' Elizabeth-Jane said.

'Oh, well. Then it's my mistake,' said Henchard. 'But the business is between me and Miss Templeman. She agrees to be my wife.'

'I do, Michael. I do,' Lucetta said weakly. 'Please don't argue about it any more.'

'There's no need for any more argument,' he said and, taking up his hat, he left the room.

Elizabeth-Jane continued kneeling by Lucetta. 'You called my father "Michael" as if you knew him well,' she said. 'How does he have so much power over you? Ah – you have so many secrets from me.'

'Perhaps you have some from me,' Lucetta replied, closing her eyes, suspecting that the secret of Elizabeth-Jane's heart concerned the man who had caused this damage to her own.

'I would never do anything to hurt you at all!' Elizabeth-Jane protested. 'I can't understand why my father is behaving so cruelly. I'll ask him to free you from your promise.'

'No, no,' said Lucetta. 'Leave things as they are.'

Chapter 8 A Narrow Escape

The next morning, Henchard went to the town hall to hear the case of a woman who had been arrested outside the church for being drunk. Despite his lack of legal knowledge, Henchard was always asked to act as magistrate whenever Doctor Chalkfield, the mayor, was absent. His experience in business and the directness of his thinking made him good at the job.

The old woman, dressed in dirty, torn clothes, stood in front of him. After Stubberd, the policeman, had told the court the main facts of the case, Henchard asked the woman if she had any questions.

'Yes,' she replied, looking at him with a strange smile. 'Twenty years ago I sold furmity in a tent at Weydon Fair. A man and a woman with a baby came into my tent. He got drunk on rum, and sold his wife and child to a sailor for five guineas ...'

While she was speaking, Henchard stared at her with fear in his eyes. He knew what she was going to say next, and he was powerless to stop her.

'... The man who sold his wife is the man sitting there in the great big chair.'

Everybody looked at Henchard, who had gone very pale.

'We don't want to hear about your life and adventures,' the second magistrate said angrily.

'But it's important to this case,' the woman protested. 'It proves that he's no better than I am, and has no right to judge me.'

'You're lying,' said the clerk. 'Be quiet, or you'll get into even more trouble ...'

'No – it's true,' Henchard said slowly. 'The old woman is right. It does prove that I am no better than she is. I cannot judge her.'

Henchard rose from his chair and left the courtroom.

News of this unbelievable development spread quickly around

the town, and soon reached Lucetta's ears. Henchard had never told her the exact details of how or why his wife had left him, and the truth shocked her. Regretting her promise to marry him, she left the house and spent the day walking around the town, thinking about what a horrible man he really was. When she returned home that evening, she told Elizabeth-Jane that she was going to Port-Breedy, a town by the sea, for a few days.

After two or three days of loneliness caused by his public shame, Henchard called to see Lucetta, and was annoyed when he learnt that she was away. He called again the next day and was informed by Elizabeth-Jane that Lucetta had returned, but she had gone for a walk along the Port-Breedy Road and would not be back until evening. After a few words of polite conversation, Henchard walked away, a thoughtful look on his face.

Lucetta, meanwhile, was walking quickly up the same road along which she had returned to Casterbridge only three hours earlier. She stopped and waited. The only building in sight was a barn. Lucetta looked into the distance and, seeing nothing, turned her face back towards the town. She was surprised to see a single figure walking in her direction – it was Elizabeth-Jane.

Lucetta seemed a little annoyed to see her, but she put on a friendly smile. 'What are you doing here?' she asked.

'I suddenly thought I would come and meet you,' Elizabeth-Jane smiled.

Before Lucetta could reply, however, she noticed something strange out of the corner of her eye. A narrow path led from the fields down to the road where they were standing – and along this path an enormous bull was walking slowly in their direction!

The animal approached, moving its head from side to side, a wooden stick swinging from a metal ring in its nose. Lucetta and Elizabeth-Jane watched nervously for a moment, then turned their backs and ran towards the only shelter they could see – the barn. This was probably a mistake because, as soon as they had turned their backs, the bull began to chase them.

The barn door was open and the two women ran straight in. They looked around desperately for somewhere to climb to safety, but they were too late. The bull ran in after them, hitting the door, which shut noisily behind it. They were trapped! As the bull ran towards them, they could feel its hot breath on their faces. With a scream, they jumped out of the way just in time and ran to the opposite end of the barn. The bull stopped, turned round and ran towards them again. Once again, the women escaped just in time. This was repeated several times, and the women were becoming more and more exhausted. They could not reach the door, and there was nowhere for them to climb. What could they do?

If the situation had continued for much longer, who knows what would have happened? But a sudden noise from the side of the barn saved them. The bull stopped, confused, as the door opened and a man appeared. Before the bull could move, the man rushed forward, caught it by the stick which hung from the ring in its nose and, with great strength, twisted its neck to one side. Blood poured from the bull's nose as the man pulled it across the floor and out of the door. Moments later the man returned, and the two women could see that it was Henchard.

He ran towards Lucetta, who was shaking with fear, took her in his arms and carried her towards the door.

'You've saved me,' she cried, as soon as she could speak.

'I've returned your kindness,' he replied gently. 'You once saved me.'

'But what are you doing here?' she asked, ignoring his reply.

'I came out here to look for you. I've been thinking, and there's something I wanted to tell you . . .'

'Not now,' she interrupted him. 'Where's Elizabeth?'

'Elizabeth?' Henchard seemed surprised, because he had not noticed his stepdaughter in his hurry to rescue Lucetta.

'I'm here,' Elizabeth-Jane announced, appearing with a smile at the door of the barn behind them.

Henchard, supporting Lucetta on one side and Elizabeth-Jane on the other, walked slowly along the road towards the town. Suddenly, Lucetta remembered that she had left her scarf in the barn, and Elizabeth-Jane offered to run back and collect it. Lucetta and Henchard walked on alone.

'Dear Lucetta,' he said, 'I'm sorry about the other night. It was wrong of me to force you to promise to marry me in that way. I realize that it would make you unhappy to marry me now, and I don't want you to be unhappy. We don't have to get married for another year or two, if that's what you want.'

'Oh, Michael, I'm very grateful to you,' Lucetta said. 'You've saved my life, but can't I thank you in another way? I'm a rich woman now. Surely I can do something more practical in return for your goodness?'

Henchard looked ahead thoughtfully. He had not expected this. 'There *is* one thing you can do for me,' he said. 'Perhaps you've heard that I've been unlucky in business this year...'

'And you'd like me to lend you some money?'

'No, no!' Henchard said, almost angrily. 'I'm not the kind of man who takes advantage of a woman's money.'

He explained how a man called Grower was demanding immediate repayment of a debt, which Henchard could not pay for another two weeks. 'I know that he'd be happy to wait for his money,' Henchard said, 'if you told him that you planned to marry me in two weeks' time. When I've got the money, I can tell him that we've decided not to get married for another year or two. Nobody else in the town will know how you've helped me, and my problem will be solved. Will you do that for me?'

'I'm sorry,' she said, looking at Henchard anxiously. 'I can't.'

'Why not?' Henchard protested. 'It isn't much to ask!'

'I can't,' she repeated, her voice rising with unhappiness, 'because... he was a witness.'

'Witness? To what?'

'He witnessed my marriage to Donald Farfrae this week in Port-Breedy.'

Henchard stood still as if he had been struck by lightning.

'I'm sorry, Michael. Please don't be angry with me...' she said quickly, alarmed by his reaction. But Henchard was not listening.

'Married him?' He finally found his voice. 'But you'd promised to marry me!'

Lucetta explained, with tears in her eyes, the circumstances which had led to her decision. 'I heard that you had sold your wife and child at a fair, like a horse or cow. How could I keep my promise after hearing that? Besides, I love Donald. I was afraid that you would tell him the secret of my past if I didn't marry him at once. You won't tell him now, will you? Promise me!'

While she was speaking, the sound of church bells and of a marching band could be heard coming from the town.

'I suppose this awful noise is to celebrate your marriage?' Henchard said bitterly.

'Yes, I think he's told them. Or Mr Grower has. I was waiting for Donald to arrive from Port-Breedy when I was attacked by that bull...'

'Then it is *his wife's* life that I've saved this afternoon.'

'Yes. And I'll always be grateful to you.'

'And what would happen if I told your husband about your past? About how you loved *me*, and wanted to marry *me*?'

'Michael, pity me. Please be generous.'

'You don't deserve pity. You did once, but not now.'

'I'll help you pay your debt.'

'Me? Receiving help from Farfrae's wife? Don't make me angrier than I am. Go away, before I say something worse.'

At that moment the marching band came into view, and

Lucetta ran away into the trees before she could be seen. Henchard did not try to stop her. He stared at the marching band from the side of the road, a wild and wounded look in his unseeing eyes.

Chapter 9   The New Master

When Lucetta told Elizabeth-Jane about her marriage to Donald Farfrae, the young girl was understandably upset. She was angry with Lucetta for not keeping her promise to marry her father, and for keeping her marriage to Farfrae a secret. But, more than this, she was unhappy because she had always believed in her heart that Farfrae would one day marry *her*. When Farfrae moved into Lucetta's house, it was too much for her. Although Lucetta wanted her to stay, Elizabeth-Jane packed her bags and moved into some small rooms in another part of town.

Henchard, meanwhile, was having problems of his own. As a result of his recent public shame, people began to stop trusting him in business. When a man who owed him a lot of money was unable to pay his debt, he realized that he was bankrupt.

He had been a foolish man, and had many other faults – but dishonesty was not one of them. He admitted his true financial position to the bank, and he lost everything he owned except for his gold watch and the clothes that he was wearing. He sold his watch and gave the last of his money to a poor farmer.

Elizabeth-Jane, who felt sorry for Henchard, tried to see him several times, but always without success. She wanted to show him that she still believed in him, although no one else did, and that she forgave him for his rough treatment of her. She wrote to him, but he did not reply. Finally, she went to his house, but discovered that he did not live there any more. He had gone to live in a small cottage owned by Jopp, his former corn manager.

When she went there, she was told that he could not be seen.

'Not even by his daughter?' she protested.

'Not by anybody – that's his order,' she was informed.

On her way home, she passed the hay barns and corn stores that used to belong to her father. She was shocked to see that the name *Henchard* had been removed, and the name *Farfrae* had been painted over it in bright, white letters.

Noticing one of her father's old workers, Abe Whittle, she asked him, 'Is Mr Farfrae master here now?'

'Yes, Miss Henchard,' the old man replied. 'He's bought the whole business. I shouldn't be saying this to you, but things are much better now. We work much harder, and we're paid less money, but we're not afraid of our new master like we were the old one. There's no more shouting or cursing at us. We're allowed to work in peace. And Mr Farfrae does things scientifically here. He measures grain with proper equipment – not like our old master, who used to do everything by guesswork. Yes, Miss Henchard, business is doing much better here now.'

Elizabeth-Jane looked at the busy activity in the yard, then turned sadly away. 'Yes,' she thought to herself. 'The old man's words are very cruel, but I'm afraid that they are true.'

Every day, Henchard went to stand alone on an old, stone bridge just outside the town. One afternoon, as he was staring into the water, Jopp – a man whom he hated but who had been the only one to offer him a place to stay – passed by.

'Mr Farfrae and his wife have moved into their new house today,' Jopp informed him.

'And which house is that?' Henchard asked, showing little interest.

'Your old one.'

Henchard looked up and saw an expression of unpleasant satisfaction on Jopp's face. 'Well, why not?' He smiled bitterly. 'He's already taken my woman and my business – why not my home too? He'll soon want my body and soul, I've no doubt.'

'No doubt,' Jopp repeated. 'If you offered it for sale.'

Satisfied that he had wounded the heart of his proud former master, Jopp went on his way.

The hours passed. Evening approached, and Henchard continued to stare down into the river in defeated silence. Then his thoughts were interrupted by another voice calling out his name. This time it was Donald Farfrae.

'I've heard that you're thinking of leaving the country, Mr Henchard,' he said to his former friend. 'Is it true?'

Henchard hesitated before replying, 'Yes, it's true. I'm going where you were going a few years ago. Do you remember how we stood like this on the bridge when I persuaded you to stay? You didn't have a penny, and I was the Mayor of Casterbridge. But now I have nothing, and you're the master of everything that once belonged to me.'

'Yes, it's strange how things happen. But I want you to listen to me just as I once listened to you. Don't go. You can come and live in your old house. I'm sure my wife wouldn't mind.'

'No, that's impossible. We'd quarrel all the time.'

'You can have your own part of the house,' Farfrae went on. 'Nobody would interrupt you. It would be healthier than down here by the river where you live now.'

Still Henchard refused. 'You don't know what you ask,' he said. 'But I thank you anyway.'

With those words, he shook Farfrae's hand and walked away.

A few days later, Henchard caught a bad cold. When Elizabeth-Jane heard this, she went immediately to his house and refused to go away until she had seen him. She found him sitting up in bed with a thick coat around his shoulders.

'Go away – go away,' he said. 'I don't want to see you.'

She refused to leave, and made herself busy tidying his room and making it more comfortable for him. She visited him every day until he was eventually well enough to go out.

When he was better, Henchard began to feel less depressed. He had been comforted by Elizabeth-Jane's visits and her loving care of him. He had also been pleased by Farfrae's thoughtful invitation for him to live in his old house. He decided it was time to do something more positive with his life, so he went to Farfrae's yard and asked for a job. He was employed at once.

For a short time, things went well. Henchard worked without complaint as a hay-packer in the yard that he had once owned. He did not see much of Farfrae, who had decided the situation was too embarrassing for frequent personal contact. But sometimes, when he saw Farfrae walk by, he stopped working for a moment and watched quietly as he went through the green door that led to the garden, and the big house, and Lucetta.

One day in early winter, Henchard heard that Mr Farfrae's name had been mentioned in the town hall as a possible future mayor, and his old feelings of bitterness returned.

'A young man of his age as mayor – it's nonsense!' he said to himself as he worked in the yard. 'But it's *her* money that's helped him. How odd it is! Here am I, his former master, working for him in his yard. And he, who used to work for me, is now my master, with the woman I was going to marry as his wife!'

He repeated these things a hundred times a day, and the other workers in the yard noticed him smiling more and more in a very unpleasant way. They also heard him more than once saying, in a voice for all to hear: 'Only two more weeks!'

'Why do you keep saying that?' a worker eventually asked him.

'Because in two weeks I'll be freed from my promise not to touch alcohol. In two weeks' time, it will be exactly twenty years since I made that promise, and I'm going to enjoy myself!'

Elizabeth-Jane was sitting at her window one Sunday when she heard Henchard's name mentioned in a conversation from the street.

'Michael Henchard's at the King of Prussia,' she heard one

man saying. 'He's drinking for the first time in twenty years.'

She jumped up, put on her things and rushed out of the door.

'That man's taken everything from me,' Henchard said, his voice thick with drink as Elizabeth-Jane led him slowly home. 'If I meet him now, I won't be responsible for what I'll do to him.'

'What will you do?' Elizabeth-Jane asked, alarmed.

Henchard did not answer, and they walked in silence until they reached the door of Jopp's cottage.

'May I come in?' Elizabeth-Jane asked.

'No, no, not today.'

Elizabeth-Jane went home, thinking about her father's drunken words and worried about what he might do. It was her duty to watch him carefully, she thought, and to protect Farfrae from any possible danger. She decided that she too should take a job as a hay-packer in Farfrae's yard.

For two or three days after her arrival at the yard, there was no sign of Farfrae. Then, one afternoon, the green door opened and Farfrae entered the yard, closely followed by Lucetta. Farfrae brought his wife forward without hesitation – he obviously still suspected nothing of her past relationship with Henchard. Lucetta, however, was unaware that Henchard was working in her husband's yard, and when she saw him she let out a cry of surprise.

Henchard raised his hat politely and continued working.

'Good afternoon,' Lucetta breathed when she had recovered from the shock.

'I beg your pardon, ma'am?'

'I said good afternoon.'

'Oh yes, good afternoon, ma'am,' he replied, raising his hat again. 'I'm glad to see you, ma'am. We poor workmen feel very honoured when a lady like you takes an interest in us.'

She said nothing, wounded by his bitter humour.

'Can you tell me the time, ma'am?' he went on.

'Half past four,' she said quietly.

'Thank you. Another ninety minutes before we're freed from work. Ah, ma'am, we poor workers know nothing of the good things of life that people of your position can enjoy.'

Lucetta smiled at Elizabeth-Jane and joined her husband at the other end of the yard.

The next morning, the postman delivered a note to Henchard:

> Will you kindly promise not to speak to me like that again? I'm glad that my husband has given you work, but please treat me as his wife and do not try to make me feel guilty. I have committed no crime, and done you no injury.

'Poor fool,' Henchard said. 'If I showed this letter to her dear husband, she would be... ha!' He gave a loud, bitter laugh and threw the letter on to the fire.

♦

As time passed, the distance between Farfrae and Henchard grew again. Henchard began to drink more heavily, but was careful to hide his increasing bitterness from his employer. Elizabeth-Jane, however, became more and more worried. She was not deceived by her father's show of friendly politeness towards Farfrae. She understood her father's wild moods and knew that, despite appearances, he could be a cruel man and a dangerous enemy.

One day, she stopped Farfrae in the street and warned him about her fears for his safety, but he refused to believe that they were serious.

'We're the best of friends,' he protested cheerfully, before continuing on his way.

Elizabeth's words, however, were not completely wasted. Farfrae thought about them, and in the end decided to do something to help his former friend regain some self-respect. He met the town clerk, and discussed the possibility of arranging for Henchard to manage a small seed shop. But he was hurt when the town clerk told him how much Henchard hated him.

'You're the only person in town who doesn't realize it,' Joyce said.

'I can't forget a man who was once a good friend to me,' Farfrae explained. 'He helped me when I had nothing, and now I want to do the same for him. But perhaps it would be better to leave the idea of buying him a shop until I've had more time to think about it.'

By that afternoon, the whole town was talking about how plans by the town hall to buy a small seed shop for Henchard had been opposed by Farfrae. When Henchard heard this, his hatred for the young Scotsman grew even more.

In the evening, when Farfrae returned home, Lucetta was puzzled by his strangely quiet mood.

'Is anything wrong?' she asked.

'It's Henchard,' he said. 'I didn't realize how much he hated me. I could understand him feeling a bit jealous, but why does he hate me so much? Can you understand it, Lucetta?'

Lucetta went pale. 'No,' she said weakly.

'I gave him a job – how could I refuse to, after the way he once helped me? But at the same time I cannot ignore the fact that he's a man with strong feelings against me. How can I trust a man who has decided to be my enemy?'

'Oh, dearest Donald, what have you heard?' Lucetta asked anxiously. The words on her lips were 'anything about me?' – but she did not say them.

'Nothing important,' Farfrae sighed.

Their conversation was interrupted by a knock on the door, and a local government official came in.

'Dr Chalkfield, the mayor, died at five o'clock this afternoon,' he announced. 'We've known that he was ill for some time, and we've been discussing things at the town hall. I've come to ask you if you would agree to be the next Mayor of Casterbridge.'

Chapter 10 The Letters

A few days later, Lucetta met Henchard by chance in the town market, and asked him to return the letters she had sent him. Henchard promised to consider her request. When she had walked away, he remembered that they were still in the dining room safe in his old house.

'I wonder if the safe has been opened?' he thought with amusement.

That evening, as the church bells rang to celebrate the election of Donald Farfrae as the new mayor, Henchard thought bitterly about recent events. Farfrae had taken everything from him – his business, his house, his wife, his position as mayor. He had even stopped him from managing a small seed shop!

'But if I show him the letters which Lucetta sent me, I can destroy their happiness,' Henchard thought, enjoying the power he had to make them suffer.

The next morning, he went to the corn yard as usual. When he saw Farfrae, he politely congratulated him on his latest success. Farfrae thanked him, pleasantly surprised by his old friend's generous attitude.

'I wanted to ask you,' Henchard went on, 'about a package that I left in my old safe in the dining room. It's not very important, but I'll call to collect it this evening, if you don't mind.'

Farfrae, who had never opened the safe, immediately agreed.

That evening, Henchard had a few drinks and then went to his old house. Farfrae invited him into the dining room, where he at once unlocked the safe and took out the package.

'I'm sorry I haven't returned them before,' he said.

'Never mind,' Henchard said, taking the package and opening it. 'They're only old letters from a woman I once knew. Do you remember I once told you about a woman in Jersey who had helped me when I was ill, and whom I had promised to marry?

Well, these letters are connected to that unhappy business. Although, thank God, it's all over now.'

'What happened to the poor girl?' Farfrae asked.

'Luckily she married, and married well, so these letters don't make me feel guilty any more. Just listen to what an angry woman can say!'

Farfrae covered a yawn, and listened politely as Henchard read one of the letters to him.

'I won't tell you her name,' Henchard said, 'as she is now another man's wife. It would be unfair of me, don't you agree?'

'Absolutely. But why didn't you marry her when your wife Susan died?'

'A good question.' Henchard smiled drunkenly. 'When I offered to marry her, she suddenly refused! She'd already married somebody else? Can you believe it?'

'Then she was not the lady for you, if she could change her affections so quickly and easily. I pity the man who married a woman like that.'

'So do I,' Henchard agreed.

He opened a second letter and began to read it aloud, unaware that Lucetta was listening to every word!

She had been reading quietly in her bedroom when she heard the doorbell ring. When she recognized Henchard's voice, she left her room and sat quietly on the stairs. Her face went white with shock when she heard that Henchard was reading out the letters she had asked him to return. After a short time, she could bear to hear no more. She returned to her room and sat on the edge of her bed, frightened that Henchard would tell her husband everything.

At last she heard the front door shutting, and the sound of her husband's footsteps on the stairs. She looked at him anxiously when he walked into the room, expecting the worst. But to her amazement, he was smiling! She was so relieved that she burst into tears.

'I'm sorry,' she said. 'It's just that everything about that man upsets me.'

'He's not the most pleasant man, I agree,' Farfrae said, comforting her without understanding the real reason behind her tears. Then he told her about Henchard's visit.

'I think he's a bit mad,' he said. 'He's been reading me a lot of letters about his past life. I don't know why . . .'

Lucetta felt confused. Why hadn't Henchard told her husband who had written the letters? She couldn't understand it. Perhaps he wanted to make her suffer before telling her husband the whole truth? She *had* to get those letters back!

The next morning, she wrote to Henchard and asked him to meet her just before sunset at the Roman ruins on the Budmouth Road.

The sun was just disappearing behind the hill when Lucetta reached the ruins that evening. She did not have to wait long. She saw a figure approach her through the shadows, then stop a short way from her. She did not know why, but she sensed something different about Henchard's attitude, even from that distance. He seemed suddenly less frightening.

She did not know the effect that her choice of time and place for the meeting had had on him. When Henchard had seen Lucetta standing in the shadows, he was reminded of another woman who had met him at the same place two years earlier – another woman whom he had treated badly and who had come to ask him for some kindness.

By the time he reached her, his heart had already melted.

'I'm sorry to see you looking so ill,' he said gently. 'Is anything the matter?'

'How can you say that? Of course something's the matter!

I heard your conversation with my husband last night. I heard you reading him my letters. Why are you being so cruel to me?'

When Henchard saw the poor, frightened woman in front of him, he felt ashamed, and he lost all desire to punish her or to take revenge on her husband.

'What do you want me to do?' he asked gently. 'I only read those letters to your husband as a joke. I didn't tell him who'd written them.'

'If you have any pity in your heart, Michael, you'll return those letters to me.'

'Of course. You can have them all. But I warn you, Lucetta, even without these letters, he's sure to discover the truth sooner or later.'

'But not before I've proved that I can be a faithful, loving wife. Then he may forgive me everything.'

Henchard looked silently at her. 'I hope so,' he said at last. 'But you'll have all your letters back. Don't worry.'

'How good you are. But how shall I get them?'

He thought for a moment, then said he would send them the next morning. 'I won't trouble you any more,' he said. 'Your secret will be safe with me, I promise.'

Returning from her appointment, Lucetta saw a man waiting by the lamp nearest to her door. When she stopped to go in, he came and spoke to her. It was Jopp.

'I've heard that Mr Farfrae is looking for a corn manager, and I'd like to offer myself for the job,' he said. 'I'd be very grateful, ma'am, if you could recommend me to your husband.'

'I don't know anything about it,' she replied coldly.

'But you can help me more than anyone, ma'am. I was in Jersey for several years, and I knew you there by sight.'

'Really?' she said. 'But I knew nothing of you.'

'A kind word from you would help me get that job.'

She still refused to become involved, and Jopp returned home an angry man. He was staring bitterly into the fire when Henchard came downstairs with a package in his hands.

'Could you do something for me, Jopp?' he asked. 'Could you take this package to Mrs Farfrae tonight? I would take it myself, of course, but I don't wish to be seen there.'

When Henchard had returned to his room, Jopp looked thoughtfully at the package on the table, wondering why Henchard did not want to return it himself. Feeling curious, he picked it up and examined it carefully. It hadn't been closed properly and, lifting one corner of the paper, he saw that it contained letters. 'I thought so,' he said to himself.

Jopp's path was by the riverside at the bottom end of the town. As he approached the bridge which stood at the end of the High Street, he saw two women he recognized – Mrs Cuxsom and Nance Mockridge.

'We're going for a drink in Mixen Lane,' they said. 'Why don't you join us?'

'All right,' he said. 'Just for five minutes.'

The pub in Mixen Lane was crowded and filled with music and laughter. Jopp stayed longer than five minutes. After he had had a couple of glasses of beer, Nance Mockridge asked him what was in the package he was carrying.

'Ah, that's a big secret,' he smiled. 'They're love letters, written by a woman of high position in this town to a man who's not her husband. Oh, how I'd love to shame her! She's so proud, I'd love to read her letters out aloud!'

'What's stopping you?' Mrs Cuxsom said. 'I'm sure we'd all love to hear them.'

Jopp opened the package carefully, picked up one of the letters and began to read.

'Mrs Farfrae wrote that!' Nance Mockridge said. 'It brings shame on all us respectable women to hear a woman of her high position writing like that. It isn't even to her husband!'

'What a good reason this is for a skimmity-ride*,' said Nance Mockridge.

'True,' Mrs Cuxsom agreed. 'We'll never have a better chance for one than this. The last one in Casterbridge was ten years ago.'

Everybody in the pub agreed, and they excitedly began making plans for the skimmity-ride. The only problem was that it cost money, and at this point the room went silent.

'Can I help you?' a voice said from the bar. Everybody looked round to see a man in a fur coat and hat, carrying an old, wooden case. 'I'm a stranger to Casterbridge,' he said. 'I'll be staying here for two or three weeks, and I'd love to see something of your ancient customs and traditions. I don't mind paying something to help you perform this skimmity-ride you're talking about. Here, good people, please accept this.'

He threw a large, gold coin on to the table.

The people in the pub thanked him for his generosity, and continued with their plans. When Jopp finally left with the packet of letters, it was too late for him to go to the Farfraes' house, so he returned home and delivered them the next day.

Within an hour, Lucetta had burnt them all. She fell to her knees, put her hands together and thanked God for making her safe at last.

Chapter 11 A Royal Visit

Life at Casterbridge was interrupted by an unexpected and

---

* skimmity-ride: an old country custom in some parts of England in the nineteenth century. Life-size models of people who had been unfaithful in marriage were carried through the town on top of a donkey.

exciting event. A member of the royal family was going to stop in the town for half an hour on his way to open an engineering factory in the west, and the townspeople decided to turn this half-hour visit into a grand occasion.

While officials in the town hall were making the final arrangements for the royal visit, their discussions were interrupted by the arrival in their room of an unexpected visitor: Michael Henchard. He stood in front of them in his dirty old clothes – the same clothes he had worn when he was mayor.

'Gentlemen,' he said, walking towards them and placing his hands on the table, 'as I am a former mayor of this town, I would like to join you when we welcome our royal visitor.'

The officials looked down in embarrassed silence and Farfrae, as the new mayor, felt it was his unhappy duty to inform Henchard that his services were not needed. Despite Henchard's protests, Farfrae refused to change his mind.

'But, of course, everybody in the town will have a good view of the ceremony,' he said. 'You can watch it like all the rest.'

Henchard left without reply. 'I'll welcome the royal visitor, or nobody will!' he said angrily to himself.

On the morning of the royal visit, people crowded into the town from miles around. The pubs opened early, and all the farmworkers put on clean shirts for the occasion. Henchard drank a glass of rum and started down the street, where he met Elizabeth-Jane.

'It's lucky I'm allowed to drink again,' he said. 'Without alcohol, I wouldn't be brave enough to do what I have to do.'

'What do you have to do?' she said, puzzled.

'Welcome our royal visitor, of course.'

'Shall we watch the royal visit together?' she suggested, alarmed by his strange behaviour.

'Watch it? I have more important things to do than that!' he said, and walked away.

Feeling worried, Elizabeth-Jane went home and changed her clothes, then came out to join the crowd outside the town hall. Behind her, some seats had been arranged on a platform for important ladies to watch the scene. Lucetta, who looked beautiful in her bright, expensive clothes, was sitting at the front. Turning round, Elizabeth-Jane could see the road along which the royal visitor would be arriving. At the front of the crowd, she noticed Henchard. He had a brightly-coloured rose in the collar of his jacket, a large flag in his hand, and was looking up at Lucetta, hoping to get her attention. But Lucetta completely ignored him. She only had eyes for her husband – the handsome young mayor with the shining gold chain around his neck. He was standing on the steps of the town hall, surrounded by an army of officials, waiting to greet the royal visitor.

The minutes passed, and the excitement in the crowd steadily increased. At last, there was a wild burst of cheering and flag-waving as the royal carriage drove slowly through the town and arrived outside the town hall in a cloud of dust.

As the carriage was slowing to a stop, a man stepped out of the crowd and, before anyone could prevent him, stood in front of it. It was Henchard. He raised his hat politely, then moved towards the carriage, holding out his hand to the royal visitor.

The ladies on the platform held their breath. Lucetta went pale and seemed ready to faint. The crowd fell silent. Elizabeth-Jane watched with a mixture of fear and curiosity, wondering what was going to happen.

Farfrae was the first person to react. He seized Henchard by the shoulder, dragged him back and told him roughly to go away. Henchard's eyes met his, and Farfrae observed the wild light in them, despite his own excitement and annoyance. For a moment, Henchard did not move, then he turned away and retired into the crowd.

The royal visitor pretended he had not noticed anything

unusual, and the ceremony continued as if nothing had happened. But for Lucetta, the event had been ruined. Everybody around her was whispering about the man in old clothes who had tried to shake hands with the royal visitor. They said that he had once helped Farfrae when the young man had nothing; if Henchard had not helped him, Farfrae would never have succeeded. Lucetta, who was unaware of the details surrounding her husband's first arrival in the town, was deeply upset.

'That's not true,' she protested loudly. 'My husband is responsible for his own success. Henchard is nothing more than a hay-cutter. If my husband weren't so kind-hearted, Henchard wouldn't even have a job!'

Henchard, meanwhile, had disappeared behind the platform where the ladies were sitting. As he stared at the part of his jacket that Farfrae had seized, he heard Lucetta deny that he had helped her husband, and say that he was only a common workman.

He went home, thinking about the injustice of Farfrae's treatment of him in public and of Lucetta's words, and met Jopp.

'So, they've treated you badly?' Jopp said. 'And in public, too? I've been treated in the same way. They're an evil couple.'

'He'll pay for this injustice,' Henchard said. 'Both of them will. I've been too gentle with them, too forgiving. I will fight him face to face – then we'll see who the real man is!'

After dinner, Henchard left in search of Farfrae. He knocked on his door and left a message for him to meet him in the barn at the back of the house. He then went round the back to the corn yard, found a piece of rope and tightly tied his left arm to his side.

'I'll show him who's strongest,' he said to himself, as he entered the barn and climbed a ladder up to the loft. 'I'll beat him with only one arm!'

Opening the loft door, he looked down into the yard and smiled. 'A drop of forty feet to the ground,' he observed with satisfaction. 'Only one of us will survive this evening!'

Henchard waited patiently. Eventually, the green door opened and Farfrae came into the yard.

'I'm up here,' Henchard called down from the loft.

Minutes later, Farfrae's head appeared through the trapdoor.

'What are you doing up here?' he asked, moving towards Henchard. 'Why aren't you on holiday like the rest of the men?'

Henchard said nothing, and turned towards Farfrae, who by now had noticed that Henchard's arm was tied to his side.

'Now,' Henchard said quietly, 'we stand face to face, man to man. Your money, wife and title are no advantage to you now, and my poverty is no disadvantage to me.'

'What are you talking about?' Farfrae asked, totally confused.

'You've stolen everything from me – my business, my woman, my title – and I have suffered it all in silence. But now you've taken something from me that I can never forgive – my pride. It was wrong of you to insult me in front of the whole town the way you did today.'

'It was your own fault,' Farfrae replied. 'You insulted a member of the royal family, Henchard. It was my duty to stop you.'

'You laid your hands on me in public,' Henchard went on, his face reddening with anger. 'Now's your chance to finish the fight you started, but this time the fight will be fair. One of us will be thrown through that door into the yard. The one who survives will be master. As the strongest man, I'll fight you with one arm. Do you understand?'

Before Farfrae could answer, Henchard had jumped at him, seized him by the collar with his free hand and tried to throw him to the floor. Farfrae fought back, and the two men stood struggling with each other, neither of them strong enough to make the other fall. Henchard forced Farfrae to his knees, but could not hold him down. He pushed him towards the open loft door, but Farfrae broke free. Then, after several minutes of this, Henchard succeeded in knocking Farfrae to the ground. Farfrae lay on his back, his head and one arm hanging out of the door, forty feet above the ground below.

'Now,' Henchard said, breathing heavily into Farfrae's face, 'this is the end of what you started this morning. Your life is in my hands.'

'Then kill me,' Farfrae said. 'It's what you've always wanted.'

Henchard stared into Farfrae's eyes, and then a change came over his face. 'Oh, Farfrae, that's not true!' he cried. 'No man ever loved another as much as I once loved you... And now, although I came here to kill you, I find that I cannot hurt you. Go and report me to the police. Do whatever you like. I don't care what happens to me now.'

Henchard rose to his feet and moved to the back of the loft, where he threw himself into a corner, filled with regret over what he had just tried to do. Farfrae got to his feet and stared at him as he brushed hay and dust from his clothes.

'I have to go to Weatherbury and Mellstock first,' he said coldly. 'When I return, I'll decide what to do.'

Then, without another word, he marched past Henchard, and climbed down the ladder into the barn.

Night fell. Moonlight filled the yard and shone through the door into the loft, where Henchard lay without moving for a long time. Then he rose to his feet and spent the next hour wandering impatiently around the town, waiting for Farfrae to return so that he could apologize. He soon found himself by the old stone bridge where he had once stood every day, staring at the river. He looked down into the moonlit water, thinking about things, wishing he was dead ...

Suddenly, he heard a strange sound coming from the centre of town. The sound of a drum, of bells, of people laughing and shouting. He looked up, wondering what it was. Perhaps it was the town band celebrating the end of an important day?

Henchard looked down at the water with a sigh. He didn't care what the noise was. He didn't care about anything any more.

Chapter 12 The Skimmity-Ride

Just before Farfrae kept his appointment with Henchard, he had received an unsigned message for him to go at once to the villages of Weatherbury and Mellstock. It had been sent by his men, who did not want him to see the skimmity-ride. They thought that if he did not see it, the skimmity-ride would fail, and nobody would be hurt. Unfortunately, they had not considered the effect of the event on poor Lucetta.

It was about eight o'clock, and Lucetta was alone by the fire, thinking about the day's events and wondering why her husband had not returned from work. Her thoughts were interrupted by the distant sound of drums and shouting, and the voice of her servant calling from an upstairs window, 'Which way are they going now?'

'They're coming up Corn Street,' a voice replied from across the street. 'They're sitting back to back, on a donkey. She's facing the head, he's facing the tail.'

'What do they look like?'

'The man's wearing a blue coat. He's got black hair and a reddish face. The woman's dressed in the same clothes that *she* wore a couple of weeks ago . . .'

Lucetta jumped to her feet. At the same moment, the door opened and Elizabeth-Jane walked towards her.

'Forgive me for not knocking,' she said breathlessly, moving quickly towards the window. She was just going to close it when Lucetta seized her by the hand.

'No,' she whispered. 'I want to see.'

She watched from the window as a crowd of people danced along the street, holding torches and laughing and singing. Then she saw the two models on the donkey.

'It's me,' she said, with a face as pale as death. 'They've made models of me, and him!'

'Let's shut it out,' Elizabeth-Jane gently suggested.

'It's no use!' Lucetta cried. 'My husband will see it, won't he? It will break his heart – he'll never love me any more – and, oh, it will kill me!'

Elizabeth-Jane put her arms around Lucetta, who watched with horror as the skimmity-ride moved slowly past her house.

'It's me,' Lucetta repeated, her body beginning to shake. 'She's wearing my clothes! She's even got my green umbrella!' She pulled away from Elizabeth-Jane and stepped back from the window, laughing madly. Elizabeth-Jane ran towards her, but she was too late. With a sudden sigh, Lucetta fell heavily to the floor.

Henchard had returned from the bridge just in time to see the skimmity-ride. He recognized the people on the donkey's back, and knew immediately what this meant. He hurried to the Farfraes' house, where he was told that Lucetta was seriously ill and a man had been sent to Budmouth to look for Farfrae.

'But he hasn't gone to Budmouth!' Henchard protested. 'He's gone to Weatherbury and Mellstock!'

Unfortunately, the people of Casterbridge had long ago lost their respect for Henchard. They thought he was just a drunk, and nobody believed him. Although Lucetta's life depended on it, no messenger was sent to Weatherbury. Henchard angrily decided that he would have to find Farfrae himself.

He ran through the town, across the open fields and up into the hills until he reached the point where the road from Weatherbury to Casterbridge turned off towards Mellstock. 'He's probably already arrived at Weatherbury,' Henchard thought. 'If I wait here, I may be able to stop him before he goes to Mellstock.'

Henchard was right. At first, as he sat in the darkness, he could hear nothing but the sound of his own heartbeat. Then he heard another sound: the sound of light wheels bumping along a stony road. Henchard ran down the hill and met the carriage just as it was approaching the turning to Mellstock.

'Farfrae!' cried the breathless Henchard, holding up his hand. 'Come back to Casterbridge at once! There's something wrong at your house, and I've run all the way here to tell you!'

Farfrae slowed the carriage. When he saw the figure waving wildly in the middle of the dark road, he suspected a trick. He thought that Henchard planned to get him alone in a dark wood, where he could easily murder him.

'I have to go to Mellstock,' he said coldly.

'I beg you!' Henchard cried. 'Your wife's ill. I can tell you all about it as we drive along...'

But Farfrae refused to listen, and drove off quickly down the road to Mellstock.

Henchard walked unhappily back to Casterbridge. When he arrived again at the Farfraes' house, he found everybody waiting anxiously for news.

'I found him,' Henchard said, sinking exhausted into a chair. 'But, like you, he didn't believe me. He won't be back for a couple more hours.'

The doctor and servants returned upstairs. Only Elizabeth-Jane stayed behind. She sat by Henchard and gently held his hand.

'So much unhappiness,' he thought, as he stared into his stepdaughter's eyes, 'but still she shows me love. I've been a fool not to notice it before.'

When Henchard got home, Jopp was waiting to speak to him.

'Somebody has called for you,' he said. 'A kind of traveller, a sea-captain, I think.'

'I don't want to see anyone,' Henchard replied, and he went upstairs to bed.

He slept badly, and at four o'clock in the morning, he got up and went out to the Farfraes' house again. A servant was standing at the door, removing a piece of cloth that had been tied around the knocker.

'Why are you taking that off?' he asked.

'You can knock as loudly as you want, now,' the servant replied. 'She'll never hear it again.'

Chapter 13 The Sailor's Return

Henchard was sitting in his room, staring at the fire, when there was a gentle knock on his door and Elizabeth-Jane came in.

'Have you heard?' she asked, a sad, pale expression on her face. 'Mrs Farfrae died about an hour ago.'

'I know,' Henchard said. 'It's so very good of you, Elizabeth, to come and tell me. You must be exhausted. Why don't you rest in the other room? I'll call you when breakfast's ready.'

To please him, and herself — because she alone among the townspeople had recognized his recent acts of kindness — she did as he suggested. While she slept, Henchard prepared breakfast. For the first time in a long time, he felt a peacefulness in his heart. He had experienced a great change of feeling towards his stepdaughter, and was honoured to have her in his house. He even dared to dream of a happy future together — two lonely people who had at last rediscovered their love for each other.

As he was watching the kettle boil with a smile of rare contentment on his lips, there was another knock on the door. He opened the door and found himself face to face with a large man of about his own age, wearing a fur coat and hat and carrying an old wooden case.

'Good morning,' the man said cheerfully. 'Are you Mr Henchard? I wonder if I could have a few words with you?'

'Of course,' Henchard said, and showed him in.

'You may remember me?' the visitor said, sitting down.

Henchard studied him for a moment, then shook his head.

'Well, perhaps not. It was a long time ago. My name's Newson.'

Henchard's face went pale. 'I know the name well,' he said quietly, looking at the floor.

'I've been looking everywhere for you, and at last I've found you. Now, about that business between us twenty years ago ...'

Henchard listened as Newson told him the story of his life with Susan and how he had pretended to drown at sea so that she would be free again to find her original husband.

'I heard that Susan is dead,' Newson said finally. 'Poor Susan, she was such a gentle, innocent woman.'

'She was,' Henchard agreed.

'But about my daughter, Elizabeth-Jane. Where is she?'

'She's also dead,' Henchard replied without hesitation. 'Surely you heard that, too?'

Newson rose to his feet with shock. 'Dead?' he repeated in a low voice. 'Then what use is my money to me now?'

Henchard shook his head without answering.

Newson walked around the room for a short time, lost in thought. Then he said, 'Where is she buried?'

'Next to her mother. She died a year ago.'

A few minutes later, Newson had gone and Henchard sat down, amazed at the lie he had just told. He had not planned it — it had seemed the natural thing to do, because he was desperate not to lose the last person in his life who could bring him happiness. But what should he tell Elizabeth-Jane when she woke up? Newson was sure to return when he discovered the truth. On the other hand, he did not want to lose her. Perhaps Newson would be so filled with grief that he would ask no more questions and never return.

While he was lost in these thoughts, Elizabeth-Jane woke up and came into the room. 'Oh, Father,' she said, rubbing her eyes, 'I've had such a long sleep.'

'I'm glad you slept so well,' he said, taking her lovingly by the hand — an act which filled her heart with joy.

The two lonely people had breakfast together, and Henchard said nothing about his visitor.

Later that day, as evening fell, Henchard was standing on the familiar stone bridge, thinking about the visit from Newson, wondering again whether or not to tell Elizabeth-Jane the truth. As he stared down at the river, he thought he saw a strange, dark shape floating in the water. Looking more closely, he saw what he thought was a human body, staring up at him with its dead, empty eyes. Henchard froze with horror when he realized that the face in the water was exactly the same as his! He was staring down at his own dead body!

He covered his eyes and ran back to town to fetch Elizabeth-Jane. She agreed willingly to go with him to the river to see what he had seen.

'What do you see?' he said, pointing over the bridge, unable to look into the water himself.

'Nothing, Father.'

'Look again more closely. Can't you see anything?'

'It looks like a lot of old clothes.'

'Are they the same as mine?'

'Yes, they are. Oh, Father, let's go away from here. I'm frightened.'

'Look at them just one more time. Then we'll go home. Tell me, what exactly can you see?'

Henchard waited while she went down to the side of the river.

When she returned, she said, 'It's the model of you they used in the skimmity-ride. They probably threw it away into the river, and it floated down here.'

'Ah, the model of me . . .' Henchard said, filled with relief. But then he had another thought. 'Where's the other model, the one of her? That performance of theirs killed her, but left me alive.'

Elizabeth-Jane kept thinking of Henchard's words – 'left me

alive' – as they walked slowly back to town. Then, without warning, she turned and threw her arms around him. 'Father, I will not leave you alone like this,' she cried. 'May I live with you and look after you as I used to? I don't mind being poor, as long as I can be with you again.'

'Oh, Elizabeth-Jane,' he said, with tears in his eyes, 'I'd like nothing more. But how will you forgive me for the rough way I treated you?'

'I've forgotten it already,' she replied.

The next morning, a farm worker discovered the models of Henchard and Lucetta in the river. They were taken out and quietly destroyed. Nobody in the town ever discussed the skimmity-ride again.

♦

At first, Farfrae was filled with grief and anger over his wife's death, and he wanted revenge. But, as time passed, his thoughts became less bitter. The tragedy had been no one's fault, he decided. The townspeople were not evil; they were just simple-minded people who had been too easily led. Besides this, Lucetta had admitted the truth about Henchard and herself just before she died. It would be better for everyone, he decided, if her past was forgotten as quickly as possible. He returned to work with renewed energy, and thought about nothing else.

When he was re-united with Elizabeth-Jane, Henchard believed he had found true happiness at last. He was even happier when Farfrae – who was always careful to avoid him – was still generous enough to arrange for him to manage the same small seed shop he had been promised earlier, before the tragedy. Life was good. By the end of the year his business had grown, thanks mainly to Elizabeth-Jane, who made many of the decisions.

When she was not working or sitting with her father in the evening, Elizabeth-Jane liked to take long walks in the country, along the Budmouth road. After one of these walks, she returned with a beautiful pair of fur gloves.

'I thought I'd buy myself a little present,' she explained when Henchard asked her about them. 'They were quite expensive, but business has been good and I thought I could afford them.'

A couple of months later, as spring was approaching, Henchard was surprised to see her room filled with new books. Although he had always wanted to encourage her to read, he had no idea that she was spending so much money on them. He decided to speak to her about this, but something happened which made him forget all about it.

One Saturday in the market, he noticed Farfrae standing, lost in thought, watching Elizabeth-Jane from a distance. Elizabeth-Jane seemed not to notice Farfrae's attention, but Henchard still became deeply worried. He had learnt to depend on Elizabeth-Jane completely, and he did not want anyone to take her away from him. He began to suspect her of meeting Farfrae when she went on her long walks along the Budmouth road, especially when he noticed that Farfrae often left town at the same time.

Once he was standing behind a wall when he heard Farfrae talking to his stepdaughter. He thought he heard him say the words 'dearest Elizabeth-Jane'. When they had gone, he followed them sadly at a distance back towards the town.

Farfrae's walks with Elizabeth-Jane were soon noticed by others, and became the subject of much conversation around town. If this had happened in the past, Henchard would have shown his anger; he would have spoken to Farfrae or forbidden his stepdaughter to go out. But he had changed. He had been defeated by life. Instead of getting angry, he just became quiet and moody. He never mentioned the subject to Elizabeth-Jane, and she never spoke to him about it.

Henchard often used to sit on a hilltop from which he had a clear view of the Budmouth road. From here, he could safely watch Elizabeth-Jane and Farfrae without being seen. One day, however, he was surprised to see a man walking slowly along the road alone. At first he thought it was Farfrae – but if this was true, where was Elizabeth? Then he saw that this man was not Farfrae at all – it was Newson!

Henchard returned home sick at heart, and found Elizabeth-Jane there.

'Oh, Father,' she said innocently, 'I've had a letter – a strange one, unsigned. Somebody has asked me to meet him this evening at Mr Farfrae's house. He said he came to see me some time ago but missed me. I didn't want to go until I had seen you. Shall I go?'

Henchard agreed with a sigh. With Newson's arrival, he knew that there was no future for him in the town.

'I'm going to leave Casterbridge,' he told her, with a calmness that surprised her.

'Leave Casterbridge!' she cried. 'And leave me?'

'You'll manage the shop perfectly well without me. I want to live in the countryside again.'

She looked down, and her tears fell silently. Eventually, she looked up and said, 'I'm sorry you've decided this. Is it because you think that I might marry Donald Farfrae?'

'It doesn't matter what I think. If you do marry him, my presence here will be very inconvenient. It's best that I go now.'

Despite her tears and protests, Elizabeth-Jane could do or say nothing to change his mind, and he left Casterbridge that evening. Elizabeth watched him go from the old stone bridge just outside the town, then walked sadly back home. On the way she met Farfrae, who took her hand and led her towards his house. She told him about Henchard's departure.

Then, as they were approaching Farfrae's house, she asked, 'Who is this man you want me to meet?'

'You'll see soon enough,' he replied, opening the door for her and showing her into the sitting room. There she saw a broad-faced man with a friendly smile sitting in an armchair. It was Richard Newson.

Elizabeth-Jane was filled with joy to see that the man she had always called 'Father' was still alive. They held each other and kissed again and again. Then Newson told her how he had known that she was living in Casterbridge, but he had not wanted to cause her any inconvenience. He had sent her money to buy books and clothes without signing his name, and he had watched her sometimes from a distance. When he told her that Henchard was not her real father, she accepted the news calmly. In fact, she was relieved to hear it, because it explained Henchard's strange behaviour towards her. And when she heard how Henchard had told Newson earlier that she was dead, she was delighted to accept Newson as her real father.

By the end of the evening, Farfrae had asked Elizabeth-Jane to marry him and Elizabeth-Jane had happily accepted.

Chapter 14 No Flowers on My Grave

Three days after the wedding, Newson left Casterbridge. Although he wanted more than anything to live near his daughter and son-in-law, he could not stay away from the sea, and returned to his small cottage in Budmouth.

The days passed happily for Elizabeth-Jane in her new life as Mrs Farfrae, but she could not completely forget her stepfather. Although she was angry with him for not telling her the truth about her real father, she began to pity him. He was homeless – possibly penniless – and she wanted to find him so that she could help him in some way. Farfrae had never hated Henchard as much as Henchard had hated him, so he agreed to help his wife in her plan.

After several days of making enquiries, he discovered that a man fitting Henchard's description had been seen a month earlier, walking towards the west along the Melchester road. He and Elizabeth-Jane left Casterbridge at once to look for him. They stopped in several villages to make more enquiries, but there was no news of him anywhere.

When they were twenty miles from Casterbridge, they decided to give up and return home. Farfrae was just turning the horses, however, when he saw an old man crossing a distant field.

'That looks like Abe Whittle,' Elizabeth-Jane said.

'It might be him,' Farfrae agreed. 'I haven't seen him at the yard for three weeks, and I owe him money for two days' work.'

They got out of the carriage and followed the old man to a small, dirty old cottage half-hidden by trees. The door was open, and Farfrae knocked. A minute later, Abe Whittle was standing before them, an empty look in his tired, sad eyes.

'Abe Whittle. What are you doing here?' Farfrae said.

'Ah, sir, you see, he was always kind to my mother, although he was often rough with me. It was my duty to look after him.'

'Who are you talking about?'

'Mr Henchard, of course. Didn't you know? He's just gone – about half an hour ago.'

'You don't mean he's dead?' Elizabeth-Jane said, putting her hands to her face.

'Yes, ma'am. He's gone. You see, I couldn't forget his kindness to my mother. I followed him out here, about the time of your wedding, and found him walking in the rain, talking to himself. He told me to go back, but I didn't listen to him. I followed him for several days until he was so ill and tired that he could hardly walk. Then I saw this empty house, and I suggested that he ought to rest. He didn't have the strength to argue, and he let me lead him here. I tried to make him as comfortable as I could, but he got weaker and weaker. Just before he died, he gave me a note.'

Whittle disappeared into the cottage for a moment, then

returned with a piece of paper, which he handed to Farfrae. On it, Farfrae read:

> I do not want Elizabeth-Jane to be told of my death.
> I do not want to be buried in church grounds.
> I do not want any bells to ring.
> I do not want anyone to see my dead body.
> I do not want flowers on my grave.
> I do not want to be remembered by anyone.
> To this, I sign my name.
> MICHAEL HENCHARD.

'What shall we do?' Farfrae asked, handing the piece of paper to Elizabeth-Jane.

'Oh, Donald,' she said at last, biting her lip with grief. 'We can't change anything. We must respect the wishes of a dead man, however sad and bitter they may be.'

From the moment she returned home, Elizabeth-Jane felt a calmness and peace in her life that she had never experienced before. She lived a life of fine clothes and comfort, but she was always aware of the important part that chance plays in our lives. To her, there was no great difference between a penniless wanderer and a mayor. Her father had been both. The strangest things can happen to anyone, and there is no reason for us to be proud of our wealth or ashamed of our poverty. There is enough beauty and pleasure in the world for everyone, even in the smallest things, if we know where to look. Happiness need not be – as she had once believed – just an occasional moment of sunlight in a long, dark life of pain.

ACTIVITIES

Chapter 1

Before you read

1 Look at the Word List at the back of the book. Check the meaning of unfamiliar words, then answer these questions. Which words refer to
   a types of transport?
   b types of building?
   c animals?
   d people?
   e emotions?

2 Read the Introduction. Are these statements true or false? Correct the false ones.
   a When he is young, Michael Henchard sells his wife to a builder.
   b Henchard stops drinking because he doesn't like alcohol.
   c Henchard becomes an important person in his town.
   d Henchard is a kind man with no faults.
   e Thomas Hardy's first successful novel was called *Desperate Remedies*.
   f Everyone loved *The Mayor of Casterbridge*.
   g Hardy stopped writing novels because his wife was angry with him.
   h Hardy's novels take place in the English countryside in the nineteenth century.
   i Hardy believed that God looks after us.

While you read

3 Complete the sentences with 1–3 words.
   a As they walk along the road, Michael and his wife do not .... to each other.
   b Michael and his wife go to a .... that is almost finished.
   c An old woman puts .... in Michael's soup.
   d Susan agrees to go with the sailor because she feels .... with her husband.

e Susan takes off her .... and throws it to her husband.
f The next morning, Michael feels very .... about his behaviour the previous night.
g He looks everywhere for his ....
h He discovers that his wife and child have ....

After you read
4 Discuss these questions with another student.
   a Is Susan right to leave her husband for the sailor?
   b Why does the sailor buy Susan?
   c Would Michael have sold his wife if he hadn't got drunk?
   d Do you feel sympathetic towards Michael in any way?

Chapter 2

Before you read
5 Discuss these questions. What do you think?
   a What does Michael do in the next eighteen years? How does his behaviour change?
   b What happens to Susan and her child?

While you read
6 Are the sentences below true (T) or false (F)?
   a Richard Newson is dead. .....
   b Susan's daughter is twenty. .....
   c Susan discovers that Henchard is a teacher in Casterbridge. .....
   d Henchard owns a wheat and corn business. .....
   e Donald Farfrae has an invention that can cure bad corn. .....
   f Farfrae agrees to be Henchard's corn manager. .....
   g Elizabeth-Jane dislikes Donald Farfrae. .....

After you read

7 Finish these sentences.
   a Susan goes to the fair because...
   b She has decided to find Henchard again because...
   c The townspeople are angry with Henchard because...
   d Elizabeth-Jane works at the hotel because...
   e Donald Farfrae is going to America because...
   f We know that Henchard likes Farfrae because...
8 What have you learnt about Donald Farfrae?
9 Discuss whether Susan is right not to tell her daughter the truth about Michael Henchard.

Chapters 3–4

Before you read

10 How will Henchard react to the news that his wife and daughter have returned, do you think? Why?

While you read

11 Who:
   a dances with Elizabeth-Jane?   ....
   b starts a small corn business outside town?   ....
   c becomes very ill?   ....
   d writes a letter to Henchard from Jersey?   ....
   e writes a letter to Henchard that must not be
      opened until Elizabeth-Jane's wedding day?   ....
   f dies?   ....

After you read

12 Answer the questions.
   a Who is Lucetta and what is Henchard's problem with her?
   b What does Henchard do that shows he is kind?
   c Why does Henchard quarrel with Farfrae? Give five reasons.
   d What does Susan tell Elizabeth-Jane about the note that was sent to her and Farfrae?
13 Describe Susan's character.

14 Discuss these questions with another student. What do you think?
   a What does Susan say in her letter to Henchard?
   b Is Henchard right to quarrel with Farfrae? Why (not)?

Chapters 5–6

Before you read
15 What will happen between these people, do you think?
   a Elizabeth-Jane and Donald Farfrae?
   b Henchard and Farfrae?
   c Henchard and Lucetta?

While you read
16 Circle the correct answers.
   a Henchard tells Elizabeth-Jane that he is her *friend/father*.
   b Henchard learns the truth about Elizabeth-Jane from a *friend/letter*.
   c Henchard starts behaving *kindly/unkindly* to Elizabeth-Jane.
   d Lucetta invites Elizabeth-Jane to *visit/live with* her.
   e Lucetta writes a letter to Henchard asking him to *visit/marry* her.
   f Donald Farfrae goes to visit Elizabeth-Jane but meets *Henchard/Lucetta* instead.
   g *Elizabeth-Jane/Henchard* guesses that Lucetta and Donald Farfrae are in love.

After you read
17 Who says or writes these words? To whom? Who or what do the words in *italics* refer to?
   a 'I'll be kinder to you than *he* was.'
   b 'On condition that you do not visit *her* in my house, I will not stand in your way.'
   c '*It* will give you an excuse to visit my house.'
   d 'Your daughter's presence may be the reason for *this* . . .'
   e '*It* will do the work with greater speed and efficiency than people can.'
   f 'Why didn't *she* trust me with *the truth*?'

18 Work with another student. Have this conversation.
  Student A: You are Lucetta. Tell Elizabeth-Jane the truth about your relationship with Henchard and your feelings for Donald Farfrae.
  Student B: You are Elizabeth-Jane. Try to hide your feelings when Lucetta talks about her feelings for Donald Farfrae.

Chapters 7–8

Before you read

19 How will the relationship between Lucetta and Donald Farfrae develop, do you think? What will the reaction of Henchard and Elizabeth-Jane be?

While you read

20 Number these events in the correct order, 1–7.
  a Henchard loses a lot of money. .....
  b Henchard threatens to tell everyone the secret of Lucetta's past. .....
  c Lucetta tells Henchard that she has married Farfrae. .....
  d There is danger from a bull. .....
  e An old woman appears at the town hall. .....
  f Lucetta refuses Henchard's offer of marriage. .....
  g Lucetta agrees to marry Henchard. .....

After you read

21 Answer these questions.
  a In what ways does Henchard behave cruelly to Lucetta?
  b What bad business decisions does Henchard make? What is the result?
  c Why does Lucetta suddenly marry Donald Farfrae?
  d What is Henchard's reaction to the marriage?
22 Describe Henchard's involvement with an old woman and how she harms Henchard.

Chapters 9–10

Before you read

23 Discuss these questions. What do you think?
   a Will Henchard tell Farfrae about Lucetta's past? If he did, what would be the result?
   b Will Henchard make money again, or will he remain a poor man?

While you read

24 Answer the questions using 1–3 words.
   a What happens to Henchard financially? ....
   b Who looks after Henchard when he is ill? ....
   c Who does Henchard start working for? ....
   d What does Henchard start doing that he has not done for a long time? ....
   e Who does Henchard read Lucetta's letters to? ....
   f Who does Henchard give Lucetta's letters to? ....
   g What does Jopp read to two town women? ....
   h What do they plan to have, to shame Lucetta? ....

After you read

25 Who says these words? Who to? Explain the situation.
   a 'There's no more shouting or cursing at us.'
   b 'You can have your own part of the house.'
   c 'We poor workmen feel very honoured when a lady like you takes an interest in us.'
   d 'Only two more weeks!'
   e 'Your secret will be safe with me, I promise.'
   f 'A kind word from you would help me get that job.'

26 Explain Henchard's bad luck when he tries to return Lucetta's letters.

27 What is your opinion of Henchard now? Why?

28 Work with another student. Have this imaginary conversation between Henchard and Farfrae.

Student A: You are Henchard. You blame Farfrae for everything bad that has happened to you. Tell him.

Student B: You are Farfrae. Tell Henchard why his problems are not your fault.

Chapters 11–12

Before you read

29 Discuss these questions. What do you think?
  a What will happen between Henchard and Farfrae?
  b How will Lucetta and Farfrae react if they see the skimmity-ride?

While you read

30 Are the sentences below true (T) or false (F)?
  a Henchard is allowed to speak to the royal visitor. .....
  b Henchard decides to fight Farfrae and try to kill him. .....
  c Farfrae almost kills Henchard. .....
  d Elizabeth-Jane prevents Lucetta from seeing the skimmity-ride. .....
  e Lucetta suddenly becomes ill. .....
  f Henchard tries to warn Farfrae about something. .....
  g Henchard agrees to see his visitor, a sea-captain. .....
  h Lucetta gets better. .....

After you read

31 Complete the sentences.
  a The town officials don't want Henchard to welcome the royal visitor because...
  b When people see Farfrae pull Henchard away from the royal carriage, they say that...
  c Henchard does not kill Farfrae because...
  d When Henchard stands by the old stone bridge he feels...
  e When Lucetta sees the skimmity-ride she is afraid that...
  f When Henchard tells people that Farfrae has gone to Weatherbury, people...
  g Farfrae does not believe Henchard because...

32 Explain how, in this part of the story:
   a Elizabeth-Jane shows her goodness.
   b Henchard shows the two sides of his character.
33 Discuss these questions with another student. Give reasons for your opinion.
   a How would you describe Lucetta?
   b Does she deserve what happens to her?
   c What is your opinion of Farfrae?

Chapters 13–14

Before you read

34 Discuss these questions. What do you think?
   a Who is the sea-captain? What part will he play in the story?
   b How will the relationship change between:
   Henchard and Farfrae?   Henchard and Elizabeth-Jane?

While you read

35 Complete the sentences with 1–3 words.
   a Henchard dreams of a happy future with ……………………… .
   b Henchard tells Newson that both Susan and Elizabeth-Jane are ……………………… .
   c Farfrae arranges for Henchard to manage a ……………………… .
   d Elizabeth-Jane starts meeting ……………………… .
   e When Newson returns, Henchard decides to leave ……………………… .
   f Farfrae asks Elizabeth-Jane to ……………………… .
   g Farfrae and Elizabeth-Jane try to ……………………… Henchard.
   h Henchard is followed by ……………………… .
   i At the end of the story Henchard ……………………… .
36 What do you know about these in this part of the story?
   a Newson's return   **c** Farfrae
   b the skimmity-ride   **d** Henchard's note
37 Answer these questions.
   a How does Henchard change?
   b What is Elizabeth-Jane's reaction to the news that Newson is her real father?
   c Why does Henchard leave?

38 Explain in your own words how Elizabeth-Jane feels at the end of the story and why.
39 Act out an imaginary conversation with another student in which Elizabeth-Jane and Farfrae discuss their feelings about Henchard's death.

Writing
40 Describe in your own words what happened in Chapter 1 at Weydon-Priors market, where Henchard sold his wife.
41 Write about the importance of one of these to the story: letters, alcohol, the weather or money.
42 Write a letter from Lucetta to a friend in Jersey who knows about the situation with Henchard and the love letters. The letter is written just before the skimmity-ride, after Henchard has agreed to return her letters. Describe Farfrae and compare him with Henchard.
43 Imagine that you are Donald Farfrae. Write paragraphs in your diary at five important points in your relationship with Henchard. Describe what is happening between the two of you and your feelings towards Henchard.
44 Imagine that you are a nineteenth-century journalist. Describe for your local newspaper the skimmity-ride in Casterbridge, and discuss whether skimmity-rides should be legal.
45 Imagine that you are Henchard. After you leave Casterbridge, you write a letter to Elizabeth-Jane apologizing for all your mistakes. Ask her to forgive you and give reasons why she should.
46 'Elizabeth-Jane is the real hero of the story.' Discuss this statement.
47 How much of Henchard's misfortune is due to bad luck, do you think? How much is due to his character?
48 Write about the novel for magazine readers. Does Hardy have a 'dark view' of life? Give reasons for your opinion.
49 Some people think that Elizabeth-Jane is too weak and allows others to control her life too much. Do you agree?

Answers for the Activities in this book are available from the Pearson English Readers website. A free Activity Worksheet is also available from the website. Activity worksheets are part of the Pearson English Readers Teacher Support Programme, which also includes Progress tests and Graded Reader Guidelines. For more information, please visit:
www.pearsonenglishreaders.com

WORD LIST

affection (n) a feeling of gentle love

aware (adj) knowing about or realizing something

bankrupt (adj) unable to pay your debts and therefore to continue in business

barn (n) a large building on a farm for keeping crops and sometimes animals in

bull (n) a male cow

candle (n) a stick of wax that gives light when it burns

carriage (n) a vehicle pulled by horses

case (n) something that must be decided in a court of law

cottage (n) a small house in the country

donkey (n) a grey or brown animal like a small horse with long ears

fair (n) an outdoor event where people show and sell goods and enjoy games and other amusements

forecast (n) a statement of what is likely to happen

grief (n) a feeling of extreme sadness, especially after someone has died

guinea (n) old British money worth a little more than a pound

harvest (n/v) the act of gathering crops from the fields

hay (n) cut, dried grass

landlady (n) a woman who owns or manages a small hotel or bar

lane (n) a narrow country road

loft (n) a room or space under the roof of a building

magistrate (n) someone who decides if people are guilty of small crimes in a court of law

mayor (n) someone who is chosen to be the head of a local council in a town or city

meanwhile (adv) while something else is happening

relief (n) the feeling that you have when you stop worrying about something

rum (n) a strong alcoholic drink made from sugar

safe (n) a strong metal box or cupboard with a lock on it, where you keep money and valuable things

sigh (n/v) to breathe out heavily, especially when you are tired or annoyed

stepdaughter (n) the daughter of your husband or wife from a previous marriage

survive (v) to continue to live after a difficult or dangerous situation

trapdoor (n) a small door that covers an opening in a floor

wagon (n) a strong vehicle with four wheels, pulled by horses